MCWP 6-12

Religious Ministry in the United States Marine Corps

US Marine Corps

To Our Readers

Changes: Readers of this publication are encouraged to submit suggestions and changes through the Universal Need Statement (UNS) process. The UNS submission processs is delineated in Marine Corps Order 3900.15_, *Marine Corps Expeditionary Force Development System*, which can be obtained from the Marine Corps Publications Electronic Library Online (http://www.marines. mil/news/publications/Pages/Publications137.aspx).

The UNS recommendation should include the following information:

- Location of change
  Publication number and title
  Current page number
  Paragraph number (if applicable)
  Line number
  Figure or table number (if applicable)
- Nature of change
  Addition/deletion of text
  Proposed new text

Additional copies: A printed copy of this publication may be obtained from Marine Corps Logistics Base, Albany, GA 31704-5001, by following the instructions in MCBul 5600, *Marine Corps Doctrinal Publications Status*. An electronic copy may be obtained from the MCCDC Doctrine World Wide Web home page: **https://www.doctrine.usmc.mil**.

**Unless otherwise stated, whenever the masculine gender is used,
both men and women are included.**

DEPARTMENT OF THE NAVY
Headquarters United States Marine Corps
Washington, DC 20380-1775

16 September 2009

FOREWORD

Marine Corps Warfighting Publication (MCWP) 6-12, *Religious Ministry in the United States Marine Corps*, describes the Chaplain Corps' philosophy of ministry in the context of the unique mission requirements of the United States Marine Corps. It provides the basis for how we train, plan, prepare, and provide for the free exercise of religion for Marines, Sailors, and their families. This publication defines the basic principles and outlines requirements for delivering religious ministry to the men and women of the Marine Corps. It provides guidance for commanders, chaplains, religious program specialists, lay leaders, and support personnel.

This publication supersedes MCWP 6-12, *Religious Ministry Support in the US Marine Corps*, dated 15 June 2001.

Reviewed and approved this date.

BY DIRECTION OF THE COMMANDANT OF THE MARINE CORPS

GEORGE J. FLYNN
Lieutenant General, U.S. Marine Corps
Deputy Commandant for Combat Development and Integration

Publication Control Number: 143 000082 00

DISTRIBUTION STATEMENT A: Approved for public release; distribution is unlimited.

PREFACE

As Lieutenant General Flynn has noted in his foreword, this publication describes the Chaplain Corps' philosophy for delivering religious ministry to the Marine Corps. This ministry is made possible by the partnership formed between the United States Marine Corps and the United States Navy Chaplain Corps, forged in freedom and tempered in the adversities faced together over two centuries of chaplains serving with Marines. This publication reflects the next steps in this partnership as the *Department of the Navy Strategic Plan for Religious Ministry* is implemented. The Commandant of the Marine Corps endorsed this plan in his September 2007 letter (appendix A of this publication), validating our core capabilities, and tasking the Chaplain Corps with transforming this plan into action on the ground. This keystone publication provides commanders and religious ministry teams a clear understanding of the purpose, mission, and principles of religious ministry and religious accommodation. This, and subsequent publications, will serve as the tools that enable chaplains and religious program specialists to continue providing the highest quality, comprehensive programs of ministry to Marines, Sailors, and their families.

Godspeed in your ministry to the men and women serving in the United States Marine Corps.

MARK L. TIDD
Rear Admiral, Chaplain Corps, U.S. Navy
Deputy Chief of Navy Chaplains
Chaplain of the Marine Corps

RELIGIOUS MINISTRY IN THE UNITED STATES MARINE CORPS

TABLE OF CONTENTS

Chapter 1. Fundamentals

Authority and Responsibility 1-1
Mission and Vision. 1-1
Free Exercise of Religion 1-1
Chaplain's Noncombatant Status 1-2
Religious Program Specialist's Combatant Status 1-2
Religious Ministry Team 1-2
Religious Ministry Team Garrison/Base Support 1-3
Religious Program Specialist Support 1-4
Marine Chaplain Assistants 1-5
Institutional Ministry in the Marine Corps. 1-5
Professional Qualifications. 1-5
Uniform Standards 1-6
Form of Address. 1-6
Code of Ethics for Navy Chaplains 1-6

Chapter 2. Organization and Administration of Religious Ministry Personnel

The Chaplain of the Marine Corps. 2-1
Marine Corps Organization 2-1
Billets and Assignments 2-3
Chaplains Religious Enrichment Development Operation. 2-5
Reserve Component Religious Ministry Team Integration 2-5
Religious Lay Leaders 2-9
Temporary Employment of Civilian Religious Ministry Professionals 2-10

Chapter 3. Religious Ministry Principles for the Marine Corps

The Mandate of Religious Ministry 3-1
Religious Organizational Endorsement
      and Command Religious Program Requirements 3-1
Mission-Essential Task List 3-1
Defense Readiness Reporting System 3-3
Religious Ministry Principles. 3-3
Confidential Communication 3-8
Pastoral/Professional Care Network. 3-9
Marine Corps Family Team Building and Other Supported Programs 3-9
Self-Care. 3-11

Chapter 4. Staff Officer Tasks

Military Organization 4-1
Officer Tasks. 4-1
Appropriated Funds Management Principles 4-4
Nonappropriated Funds. 4-5
Material Readiness and Accountability 4-5
Command Religious Program Tables
of Equipment and Property Accounts. 4-5
Command Religious Program Facilities 4-5
Community Relations Projects 4-6
Authority to Sign "By Direction" 4-6

Chapter 5. Core Capabilities

Religious Accommodation: Facilitation and Provision 5-1
Pastoral Care 5-3
Advisement 5-5
Guidance on Public Prayer 5-6

Chapter 6. Combat Ministry Readiness

Formation: Establishing the
Religious Ministry Team for Combat Operations. 6-1
Coordinated Efforts Between Commands. 6-2
Component Religious Ministry. 6-2
Planning: Develop the Religious Ministry Estimate Situation 6-2
Tasks for Command and Supervisory Chaplains 6-3
Basic Predeployment Preparations 6-3
Deployment/Employment 6-8
Nongovernmental Organizations Support. 6-10
Crisis Response or Limited Contingency Operations. 6-11
Religious Support to Civil Affairs
and Humanitarian and Civic Assistance Operations. 6-11
Peace Building 6-12
Postdeployment Programs. 6-12
Marine Corps Combat Operational Stress Control Program 6-13

Chapter 7. Training, Professional Military Education, and Resource Support

Professional Competence and Training 7-1
Naval Chaplains School Courses 7-1
Chaplain Corps Officer Training 7-1
Religious Program Specialist Training 7-2
Training and Readiness Manual 7-2
Chaplain and Religious Program
Specialist Expeditionary Skills Training Course 7-2
Command Religious Program Personnel Training 7-3

Ecclesiastical/Religious Qualifications 7-3
Command and Staff College Distance Education Program 7-3
Joint Training 7-4
Fleet Marine Force Qualified Officer Program 7-4
Navy Enlisted Fleet Marine Force Warfare Specialist Program 7-4
Armed Forces Chaplains Board 7-4
Naval Support Branch, Logistics Integration
Division, Capabilities Development Directorate, MCCDC 7-5
Training and Education Command, MCCDC 7-5
Navy Knowledge Online 7-5

Appendices

A   Commandant of the Marine Corps Memorandum A-1
B   Reserve Mobilization Process for
Reservists on Unit Table of Organization B-1
C   Survey: US Marines' Expectations of Operational Chaplains C-1

Glossary

References and Related Publications

CHAPTER 1
FUNDAMENTALS

Authority and Responsibility

This publication sets forth the United States Marine Corps' doctrine of religious ministry. The principles and doctrine contained in this publication constitute the formal authority and assignment of implementation responsibilities to all commanders by the Commandant of the Marine Corps (CMC). It has been prepared in accordance with policy as set forth by the Secretary of the Navy Instruction (SECNAVINST) 1730.7D, *Religious Ministry Support Within the Department of the Navy*; Marine Corps Order (MCO) 1730.6D, *Command Religious Programs in the Marine Corps*; and SECNAVINST 1730.9, *Confidential Communications to Chaplains*.

Guidance in this publication requires judgment in its application. Chaplains are encouraged to focus their role in the accommodation and delivery of religious ministry, to include advising the commander as set forth in SECNAVINST 1730.7D, and related instructions. Guidance provided in this publication should be followed, except when, in the judgment of the commander, exceptional circumstances dictate otherwise. Most of the content is applicable for garrison, base ministry, and operational ministry, unless specifically noted.

Mission and Vision

The mission of religious ministry in the Marine Corps is to deliver religious accommodation, care, and advisement in order to strengthen faith, values, and virtues, so that Marines, Sailors, and their families may best serve their country. Religious ministry teams (RMTs) (comprised of a chaplain and religious program specialist [RP])

provide the following four capabilities to accomplish this mission:

- *Facilitate.* Chaplains and RPs are trained and certified to manage and execute command religious programs (CRPs) that accommodate diverse religious requirements.
- *Provide.* Chaplains meet faith group specific needs, including worship services, rites, religious and/or pastoral counsel, scripture study, and religious education. Religious program specialists are uniquely trained to support religious accommodation.
- *Care.* Chaplains, supported by RPs, deliver specific institutional care, counseling, and coaching that attends to the personal, spiritual, and relational needs beyond a faith group specific context.
- *Advise.* Chaplains advise commanding officers on issues relating to morals, ethics, spiritual well-being, and morale. Within the boundaries of their noncombatant status, chaplains advise on the impact of religion on operations. Chaplains and RPs train and educate leaders at all levels in moral decisionmaking, cultural awareness, and cross-cultural communications.

The overarching vision and outcome for RMTs is to ensure that Marines, Sailors, and their families are mission ready—demonstrating spiritual, moral, and ethical maturity, supported by the innovative delivery of religious ministry and compassionate pastoral care.

Free Exercise of Religion

Marine commanders are responsible for the free exercise of religion and religious support programs within their units. Navy chaplains and RPs serve with Marines and Sailors to assist and advise in the primary duty of providing for religious rights in accordance with Service directives.

The Constitutional protection of free exercise of religion for Marines and Sailors is clearly outlined and provided for by—

- *United States Code, Title 10, Armed Forces,* Chapter 555, Section 6031, Chaplains: Divine Services, requires commanders to cause divine services to be performed and protects the chaplain's ability to conduct those services "according to the manner and forms" of the chaplain's religious organization.
- Department of Defense Instruction (DODI) 1300.17, *Accommodation of Religious Practices Within the Military Services,* outlines the same concepts for religious freedom in the Armed Services.

Navy chaplains are qualified religious ministry professionals (RMPs) of the Department of Defense (DOD) who have been endorsed by the DOD's recognized religious organizations to provide religious ministry to the sea services. Their ministry, with the assistance of the RP, serves to promote the spiritual, religious, ethical, moral, corporate, and personal readiness of Marines, Sailors, family members, and other authorized persons consonant with their rights and needs, thereby enhancing unit readiness and increasing mission accomplishment in the Marine Corps.

Chaplain's Noncombatant Status

In accordance with SECNAVINST 1730.7D and MCO 1730.6D, US chaplains are forbidden to carry weapons. In addition, according to Department of the Navy (DON) policy, bearing arms is incompatible with a chaplain's religious functions and spiritual duties. An individual chaplain who violates this policy endangers the noncombatant status of all other chaplains.

The Geneva Conventions of 1949 accord a special protective status to chaplains. Pursuant to the Geneva Conventions, chaplains are exempt from being treated and retained as prisoners of war, and they are permitted to carry out their religious duties after falling into enemy hands. Unless their retention by the enemy is required to provide for the medical or religious needs of prisoners of war, chaplains must be repatriated at the earliest opportunity. To be entitled to this immunity, chaplains must, at all times, avoid any activity that compromises their noncombatant status per *United States Navy Regulations,* 1990, Article 1063.

Religious Program Specialist's Combatant Status

Religious program specialists are combatants with the role of providing force protection and physical security for the RMT. It is recommended that RPs receive training in provision of physical security, such as the Marine Corps Martial Arts Program.

Religious program specialists carry arms and are required to train and be proficient with their table of organization (T/O) weapon. According to MCO 3574.2K, *Marine Corps Combat Marksmanship Programs,* RPs are required to qualify with their weapon. The T/O weapons qualifications currently state that E5 and below qualify on the service rifle, and E6 and above qualify with the service pistol with the option of also qualifying with the service rifle.

Religious Ministry Team

The RMT is the commander's primary resource for the delivery of comprehensive religious ministry for operational, garrison, and/or base CRPs. Chaplains, RPs, and other designated command members (e.g., assistants, civilian contract staff, appointed lay leaders) form the RMT. However, the RMT is mainly the chaplain and RP team, whose primary duty is the delivery of the four core religious ministry capabilities listed in the Mission and Vision paragraph on page 1-1.

The composition of each command's RMT will be determined by the command's mission and T/O. Every unit is entitled to, and provided, religious support. When a unit does not have an organically assigned RMT, religious support is provided by the RMT assigned by higher headquarters. When this is not possible, other options for obtaining professional personnel resources from beyond the command include Navy chaplains from other units, chaplains of other area military or coalition services, Selected Reserve chaplains or voluntary training unit (VTU) chaplains, contract civilian clergy, and lay leaders. All RMTs serving in operational and forward deployed units should refer to chapter 6 for guidance on establishing the RMT for combat operations.

Religious Ministry Team Garrison/Base Support

The RMTs deliver direct support to the base commander for a comprehensive CRP. These duties include, but are not limited to—

- Providing religious support for all authorized Marines, Sailors, and civilians on the base.
- Preparing Marines, Sailors, and their families before, during, and after military operations and deployments.
- Supporting RMT training and readiness.
- Initiating and maintaining liaison with local community resources.

Deliver Religious Support

The Marine Corps base (MCB) chaplain is responsible to the base commander for all religious support on the base, including all religious services and activities. The base RMTs provide a broad religious support program for units,

Marines, Sailors, and their families. Worship services, pastoral care, religious education, and spiritual fitness training are provided for the religious support needs of local authorized personnel. Proper coordination with tenant units is required to ensure comprehensive implementation of the CRP. If the base has a Chaplains Religious Enrichment Development Operation (CREDO), a close cooperative relationship should be established between CREDO and base RMTs.

Provide Required Operational and Deployment Assistance

The RMTs are a primary resource to base commanders for assisting families of deployed personnel. Wounded Marines and Sailors and their families require specialized pastoral care and increased support. The RMTs are encouraged to work closely with base resources, to include Marine Corps Community Services (MCCS) and other agencies (see chap. 3). Additionally, RMTs offer predeployment and postdeployment warrior transition (WT) program support to Fleet Marine Force (FMF) units.

Support RMT Training and Readiness

All RMTs are required to be trained and prepared to implement religious support mission of the commander in any contingency. Spiritual readiness is essential to sustain Marine and Navy families while the unit is deployed. It is also essential to train RMTs while in garrison in preparation for being called as individual augmentees (IAs) and to sustain them between operational command assignments. Base RMTs will also be called upon to support drilling Reserve RMTs and for integrating Reserve Component annual training and command inspections.

Training is the critical component in preparation for military operations. The base chaplain should ensure that all RMTs under his supervision receive all unit training provided by the S-3/G-3 and through applicable Chaplain Corps and local civilian training opportunities especially related to pastoral care of Marines, Sailors, and their families.

Religious ministry teams should participate in both unit and religious support training to ensure their tactical and technical proficiency. If training for either operational or base settings is neglected, RMTs will not be adequately prepared to provide comprehensive religious support to those for whom they are responsible.

Initiate and Maintain Liaison with Local Community Resources

Beyond a sound working relationship with local civilian religious leaders, it will be necessary to initiate and maintain liaison with local community resources. Social service agencies in the community that provide counseling services, donations of food and clothing, and emergency aid for crisis or disaster situations are valuable resources for referrals.

Religious Program Specialist Support

Religious program specialists are uniquely trained and qualified Sailors assigned, along with chaplains, to support the delivery of religious ministry. As enlisted and nonordained members of the RMT, the RPs' responsibilities focus on facilitation of religious ministry support—including accommodation, provision, care, advisement support, RMT force protection, logistics, program management, and administration. Chaplains should fully utilize the particular gifts and talents that individual RPs bring, thereby multiplying the strength of the team.

Religious program specialists organizationally report to the chaplain and receive enlisted leadership and direction from Navy senior enlisted staff members (e.g., regimental battalion aid station) and Marine Corps senior enlisted staff members

(e.g., sergeant major, 1st sergeant, company gunnery sergeant, S-1 staff noncommissioned officer) for training and accountability purposes. This cooperative support is especially critical for junior RPs to ensure balanced development as an FMF Sailor. General duties of RPs serving with the Marine Corps, in addition to providing security for the RMT, include—

- Providing combat field ministry support, to include coordination of convoy logistics and force protection, host nation religious leader engagement, and advising on religious ministry support.
- Preparing and "rigging" facilities used for religious services and programs in the field and garrison; operating audiovisual equipment; and coordinating activities in support of worship services, religious education programs, spiritual renewal activities, foreign humanitarian assistance, civil support, and community relations projects; and performing other military duties as required.
- Providing general troop referral and assistance.
- Identifying and responding to Marines and Sailors experiencing combat operational stress.
- Performing triage for ministry in a mass casualty event.
- Maintaining records and reports—including facility and equipment reports and records—and updating documents, directives, and instruction files.
- Conducting inventories, safeguarding and maintaining equipment, managing the operational ministry budget, assisting in the management of the Religious Offering Fund (ROF), ordering supplies, and preparing maintenance requests.
- Providing administrative and logistical support at ceremonies and sacraments—including weddings, funerals, memorial services, baptisms, and special religious services and activities.
- Maintaining the RMT's table of equipment (T/E) and mount-out supplies in preparation for embarkation.

- Performing regularly scheduled preventive maintenance on assigned vehicles and equipment.
- Performing other duties as assigned by the chaplain.

Marine Chaplain Assistants

When RPs are not available to be assigned to units with assigned chaplains, the commander will have an incomplete RMT. Therefore, it is expected that qualified Marines with a military occupational specialty (MOS) of 0151 be assigned to serve as Marine chaplain assistants (CAs). They will work directly for the chaplain to whom they have been assigned. Chaplain assistants are expected to perform the same duties as RPs, including adhering to confidentiality privileges. The commander and chaplain will ensure that any required training is provided. Additionally, a commander may desire to assign a Marine CA for other needs, including but not limited to, augmenting driving of and personnel protection for the RMT while traveling in theater.

Institutional Ministry in the Marine Corps

The Marine Corps, like the American society from which it is drawn, is pluralistic in that faith groups and religious organizations coexist in mutual respect. Because of the impracticality of providing RMPs reflecting every religious organization on each ship, station, or base, the DON and the religious organizations of the United States have developed an institutional ministry that provides both cooperative and cooperating ministry. Every RMT must be willing and able to function in a pluralistic environment, where diverse religious traditions exist side-by-side with tolerance and respect. Chaplains and RPs are specialists trained to accommodate religious requirements and deliver ministry within the demanding and specialized military environment, without compromising the tenants of their own religious tradition and organization.

As stated in SECNAVINST 1730.8B, *Accommodation of Religious Practices*, this policy implies that the commander will—

- Make provisions to accommodate the religious needs of every member of the command within these limits.
- Acknowledge that each command may be affected by different conditions and require individual consideration of special requests for religious accommodation.

Professional Qualifications

The two aspects of a Navy chaplain's role are the chaplain's identity as an endorsed representative of a religious organization and the chaplain's identity as a commissioned Navy staff officer.

In the act of endorsing their RMPs for naval commissions, the religious organizations of the United States concede that—

- The RMPs will be placed under military command.
- The RMPs will be subjected to military regulations and directives.
- The RMPs accept the principle of command responsibility for the spiritual and moral welfare of naval personnel.
- The RMPs accept the necessity of cooperative ministry.

Religious organizations, by endorsing chaplains, support Marines, Sailors, and their families' free exercise of religion in the sea services. Religious organizations retain their responsibility to mentor, develop, and hold chaplains accountable for their professional and personal competencies.

While chaplains may possess professional credentials—such as educational degrees or state credentials as clinical counselors, physicians, and psychologists—chaplains are assigned only as

RMPs and commissioned staff officers. The maintenance of religious endorsement credentials is the official responsibility of each chaplain.

The Chief of Navy Chaplains has the responsibility to serve as liaison with endorsing agents and religious organizations regarding professional credentials and other administrative matters that are related to ministry requirements, expected competencies, and other needs or expectations of the Navy. Chaplains are expected to maintain all required relationships with their religious organization's endorsing agent and communicate with them on a regular basis. Chaplains may attend conferences sponsored by their endorsing agent, but are not authorized to contact endorsing agencies regarding other chaplains.

Chaplains assigned to the Marine Corps are expected to use their professional qualifications to deliver religious accommodation and support to the men and women serving in the Marine Corps, their family members, and authorized personnel. MCO 1730.6D provides specific guidance for outside employment or religious obligations by chaplains.

Uniform Standards

Uniform, grooming, and appearance standards are prescribed for Navy personnel serving with the Marine Corps in MCO P1020.34G, w/chs 1-5, *Marine Corps Uniform Regulations.*

Navy enlisted personnel are given the option to wear identified Marine Corps uniforms when assigned to a Marine Corps unit. Enlisted Sailors opting to wear Marine Corps uniforms are authorized to be issued and wear the Service Dress A, B, and C uniforms. Sailors exercising this option sign an agreement to observe Marine Corps uniform regulations that require adherence to the grooming and physical readiness standards of the Marine Corps. Sailors who do not take the Marine Corps uniform option will maintain Navy grooming and appearance standards. Chaplains may also purchase and wear the same uniforms, with the understanding that they will observe the same standards dictated by that uniform.

Form of Address

In verbal or written communications, chaplains are addressed in accordance with *United States Navy Regulations,* 1990. Within the military community, chaplains of all ranks are addressed and introduced properly by the term, "Chaplain." Terms of address that are common within particular faith groups or denominations (e.g., Father, Pastor, Rabbi, Imam) may also be used in addressing the chaplain.

The religious ministry specialists are to be addressed as either "RP (rank), last name" (e.g., RP2 Jones) or "Petty Officer, last name" (e.g., Petty Officer Jones). Chief petty officers and above are to be addressed by their rank rather than rating (e.g., Chief Jones, Senior Chief Jones, Master Chief Jones).

Code of Ethics for Navy Chaplains

Chaplains have a responsibility to practice ministry within a cooperative framework of respect for others, recognizing the diverse pluralistic environment in which they are called to function. While not prescriptive, a Code of Ethics for Navy Chaplains, adapted from national religious advisory groups, has often been quoted and remains a sound reference point for ethical reflection by chaplains.

Code of Ethics for Navy Chaplains

1. I will hold in trust the traditions and practices of my religious body.

2. I will carefully adhere to the directions conveyed to me by my endorsing body for maintenance of my endorsement.

3. I understand, as a Navy chaplain, I must function in a pluralistic environment with chaplains and delegated representatives of other religious bodies to provide for ministry to all military personnel and their families entrusted to my care.

4. I will provide for pastoral care and ministry to persons of religious bodies other than my own as together we seek to provide the most complete ministry possible to our people. I will respect the beliefs and traditions of my colleagues and those to whom I minister.

5. I will, if in a supervisory position, respect the practices and beliefs of each person I supervise. I will, to the fullest extent permissable by law and regulations, exercise care not to require of them any service or practice that would be in violation of the faith and practices of their particular religious body.

6. I will hold in confidence any privileged communication received by me during the conduct of my ministry. I will not disclose confidential communications in private or public.

7. I will model personal integrity and core values.

CHAPTER 2
ORGANIZATION AND ADMINISTRATION
OF RELIGIOUS MINISTRY PERSONNEL

The Chaplain of the Marine Corps

The Chaplain of the Marine Corps reports directly to the CMC and serves on the CMC's staff. This chaplain flag officer also serves as the Deputy Chief of Navy Chaplains, reporting to The Navy Chief of Chaplains. The Chaplain of the Marine Corps advises the CMC and Headquarters, Marine Corps (HQMC) staff agencies on all religious ministry matters throughout the Marine Corps (MCO 1730.6D). The Chaplain of the Marine Corps is responsible for the staffing requirements for chaplains and RPs within the Marine Corps and advises the Total Force Structure Division, Marine Corps Combat Development Command (MCCDC) regarding billet placement, quality, and staffing levels for chaplains and RPs.

Marine Corps Organization

Chaplains and RPs should have a basic understanding of Marine Corps organization if they are to carry out their duties effectively. The Marine Corps is focused on major conflicts and campaigns, as well as smaller scale stability operations that are a part of humanitarian and civic assistance (HCA) or civil affairs. Therefore, RMTs may find themselves ministering around the globe in various types of Marine Corps organizations.

As depicted in figure 2-1, on page 2-2, the President and/or the Secretary of Defense direct the Secretary of the Navy and the CMC. Combatant commanders (CCDRs) then direct or communicate with Marine Corps component commanders (see the Operating Forces paragraph).

Expeditionary in nature, the Marine Corps is organized as a "force-in-readiness" that is able to support a wide range of national military requirements. Deploying for combat as a combined-arms Marine air-ground task force (MAGTF), the Marine Corps provides the President and the Secretary of Defense with a responsive force that can conduct operations across the full range of military operations. The Service is divided into four broad categories—HQMC, operating forces, supporting establishment, and reserves.

Headquarters, Marine Corps

Headquarters, Marine Corps consists of the CMC and those staff agencies that advise and assist him in discharging his responsibilities. The Chaplain of the Marine Corps is a staff officer reporting directly to the CMC and the Assistant CMC.

Operating Forces

Operating forces are the heart of the Marine Corps; they comprise the forward presence, crisis response, and fighting power that the Marine Corps makes available to US unified CCDRs. The Marine Corps has permanently established two component commands that consist of permeanantly assigned forces—the United States Marine Corps Forces Command (MARFORCOM) and the United States Marine Corps Forces, Pacific (MARFORPAC). Normally, these forces are task-organized for employment as a MAGTF. The largest form of the MAGTF is the Marine expeditionary force (MEF).

Marine Corps forces (MARFOR) commanders are responsible for coordinating and integrating religious ministry within their operational area. The MARFOR chaplains advise the MARFOR

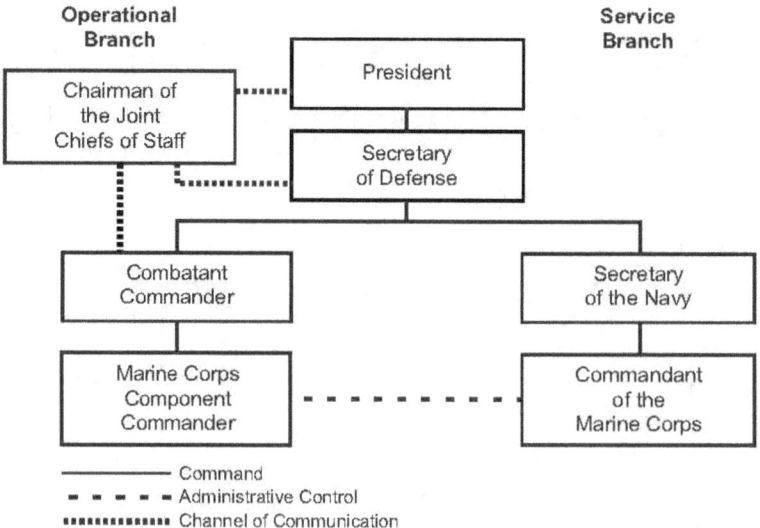

Figure 2-1. Marine Corps Operational and Service Branches.

commanders on matters relating to the religious, spiritual, moral, and ethical readiness of assigned forces and individual commands.

Marine Expeditionary Force

The MEF is the principal Marine Corps warfighting organization. It is composed of a logistics combat element (LCE) (logistic group), ground combat element (GCE) (division), and an aviation combat element (wing). The MEF is capable of conducting missions across the range of military operations through amphibious assault and sustained operations ashore, in any environment.

The MEF commander is responsible for coordinating and integrating religious ministry within his operational area. The MEF chaplain is responsible for managing religious ministry requirements and ensuring the religious ministry established by MEF major subordinate commands (MSCs) form an integrated and responsive network of support. The MEF chaplain and religious ministries staff also advise the MEF commander on matters relating to the religious, spiritual, moral, and ethical readiness of the command; religious ramifications affecting mission; religious ministry

logistics; and current and future religious ministry plans and staffing at the MEF level. Components of the MEF are the—

- Marine division (MARDIV).
- Marine aircraft wing (MAW).
- Marine logistics group (MLG).

Marine Division

The MARDIV is a ground force of combat and combat support units organized and equipped primarily for amphibious and ground operations. It consists of three infantry regiments, an artillery regiment, and separate combat support battalions. Subordinate units can be organized into effective forces of combined arms based upon the infantry regiment, infantry battalion, or tank battalion. One or more division(s) forms the GCE of the MEF. To perform its combat role, the MARDIV requires air defense and aviation support from a MAW and Service support from an MLG.

The chaplain and religious ministry staff of the MARDIV are similar to the MEF's staff but are more specifically related to the activities of the GCE. When units smaller than divisions deploy as the GCE, the regiment or battalion chaplains assume much of the planning responsibility associated with their respective units.

Marine Aircraft Wing

The MAW is the highest level of aviation command in the FMF. The MAW is task-organized to provide a flexible and balanced air combat organization capable of providing the full range of combat air operations in a variety of areas, without the requirement of prepositioned support, control, and logistic facilities. Only the wing has the inherent capability of performing all six of the Marine aviation functions—antiair warfare, offensive air support, assault support, electronic warfare, air reconnaissance, and control of aircraft and missiles—in support of the MAGTF.

Each MAW has a unique organizational structure that includes a MAW headquarters, several Marine aircraft groups, a Marine air control group, and a Marine wing support group. The Marine wing support squadron provides aviation ground support for all supporting or attached units of the Marine air control group. The RMTs are assigned to each of these units. The MAW chaplain is responsible to the commander of the MAW and tasked with supervision of the RMTs in the squadrons and groups.

Marine Logistics Group

The MLG is the LCE of the MEF. It is a permanently organized command charged with providing combat service support beyond the organic capabilities of supported units of the MEF.

The MLG chaplain advises the commander on the religious, spiritual, moral, and ethical readiness of the command and the adequacy of religious ministry support throughout the MLG. The RMTs in MLG units work very closely with medical units while deployed. In garrison, the RMTs work with all units to ensure adequate delivery of religious ministry.

Supporting Establishment

The Marine Corps supporting establishment consists of those personnel, bases, and activities that support the Marine Corps' operating forces. This infrastructure consists primarily of 15 major bases and stations in the United States and Japan. It also includes the Marine Corps Recruiting Command, MCCDC, and the Marine Corps Logistics Command, as well as all training activities and formal schools. The supporting establishment also provides facilities and support to the families of deployed Marines, allowing Marines to concentrate on their demanding missions. The RMTs are assigned throughout these commands to ensure adequate delivery of religious ministry.

Reserves

The United States Marines Corps Forces, Reserve (MARFORRES) is organized, trained, and equipped under the direction of the CMC and commanded by the Commander, MARFORRES. Units of this command have been closely integrated with the Active Component under the Marine Corps' Total Force Structure concept. The MARFORRES shares the same commitment to expeditionary readiness as the active duty Marine Corps.

Further guidance on how the Marine Corps is organized may be found in Marine Corps Reference Publication (MCRP) 5-12D, *Organization of Marine Corps Forces*; Marine Corps Doctrinal Publication (MCDP) 1-0, *Marine Corps Operations*; and the current *United States Marine Corps Concepts and Programs* publication. Figure 2-2, on page 2-4, is an overview of how the forces are structurally organized.

Billets and Assignments

Chaplains are commissioned as Navy officers with the understanding that they can be assigned to serve with the Marine Corps. Religious

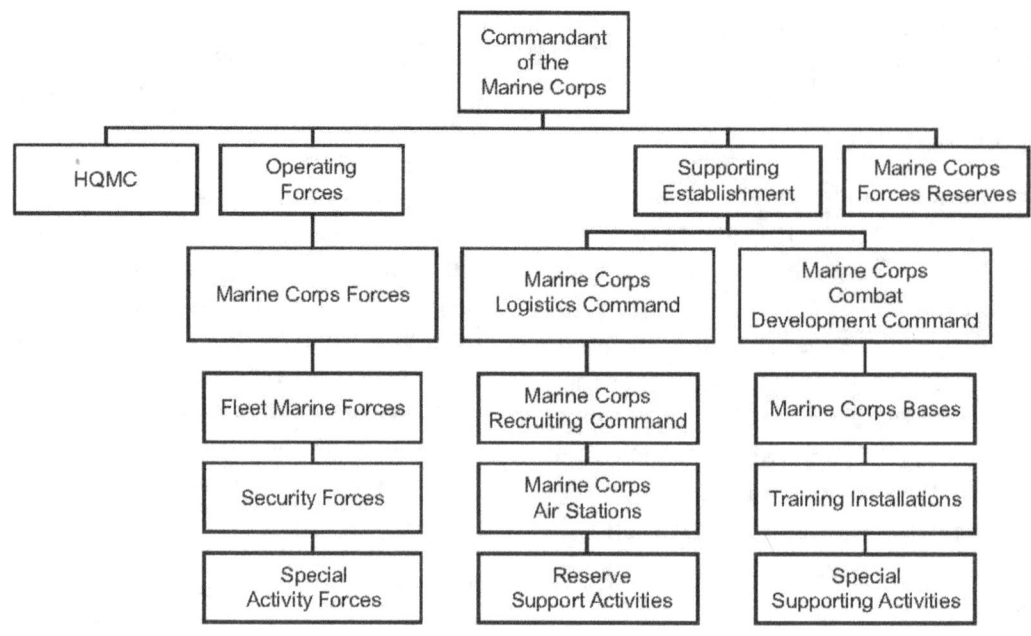

Figure 2-2. Marine Corps Organization.

program specialists sign a statement of understanding that they are required to serve with the Marine Corps as combatants, if assigned, based on the needs of the Navy and Marine Corps. Chaplains and RPs are assigned to the Marine Corps with the understanding that they are required to comply with the unique requirements and standards for Navy personnel serving in the Marine Corps. In Marine commands where the T/O has more than one chaplain and RP, the command chaplain advises the commander concerning the placement and assignment of all chaplains and RPs within the command. Assignments are made in accordance with the command's T/O. Commands ensure that the Marine T/Os and Navy Activity Manpower Document (AMD) are reconciled. Staffing levels are regularly reported to the Chaplain of the Marine Corps, who ascribes billets according to inventory of RMT assets and the needs of commands. Navy chaplains and RPs are assigned to Marine Corps commands by written orders from the Naval Personnel Command, according to the Marine Corps' T/O and Navy AMDs. Each Marine Corps command's

Navy AMD lists chaplain and RP billets corresponding to the T/O. The Total Force Structure Division, MCCDC, ensures Marine and Navy structure and manpower documents correctly reflect the validated requirements in accordance with MCO 5311.1C w/ch 1, *Total Force Structure Process (TFSP)*.

Deployable commands (MARFOR) have the highest priority in billet placement and staffing authorization to ensure that direct religious ministry requirements for expeditionary forces are met. Billet placement for operational support commands (i.e., training commands and bases) are structured to ensure direct religious ministry is provided for all Marines, Sailors, and their family members.

The force chaplains of MARFORCOM, MARFORPAC, and MARFORRES regularly report chaplain and RP staffing levels to the Chaplain of the Marine Corps. Authorized manning levels are monitored by the Chaplain of the Marine Corps to ensure the required religious ministry is being provided.

Chaplains Religious Enrichment Development Operation

The CREDO program, instituted in 1971, exists on both Navy and Marine Corps installations, and it remains a core program designed to aid the Chaplain Corps in the performance of their duties. The CREDO program's mission is to develop and provide briefs, seminars, and retreats that will ensure Marines, Sailors, and their families are healthier, more resilient, and better prepared for war and peacetime demands and stresses. Chaplains and Personal Growth Retreat team members work with participants in retreat group settings to achieve positive results through supportive interaction within the CREDO. The 72-/48-hour retreats are designed to improve relationships, resolve issues, and develop personal and spiritual resources—all known to be factors in improving resilience. The CREDO program offers personal growth, marriage enrichment, spiritual growth, and family-oriented retreats. In addition, the CREDO program offers warrior preparation, transition, and reintegration briefs if a unit chaplain requests CREDO's assistance. Each center has the flexibility to design programs that meet the greatest need, such as one-day marriage seminars or singles seminars offered within the individual command. The CREDO program is available at all three MEFs and in Hawaii. Program funding for the CREDO program at Marine Corps installations is provided by MCCS.

The Chief of Chaplains is the program sponsor for all CREDOs. The CREDO program provides an assortment of ministries and weekend retreats primarily to active duty Service members and their family members and secondarily to Reservists and their family members and retired, DOD, and Civil Service personnel. Programs are operationally focused, family supportive, and flexible in the provision of ministry. The mission of the CREDO program is to help people mature toward an increased functional ability, acceptance of responsibility, and resilience within all areas of life.

Reserve Component Religious Ministry Team Integration

Reserve Component chaplains and RPs are valuable and proven religious ministry assets for the Marine Corps. Smooth and successful Active and/or Reserve integration requires an understanding of the types of Navy Reserve (NR) units, personnel qualifications, responsibilities of each associated command, categories of Reserve training, forms of operational support available to assist the Active Component, mobilization processes, and the proper professional care of Reserve personnel.

There are two major categories of Reserve Component chaplain and RP billets that support the Marine Corps:

- *Commissioned units.* Chaplain and RP billets are organized within NR units that support Selected Marine Corps Reserve (SMCR) commands of MARFORRES. The SMCR units closely "mirror" similar Active Component units in mission and composition of RMT billets. These NR units are also composed of medical personnel and may include naval gunfire personnel. The commanding officer of the NR unit is usually a medical officer. Personnel assigned to these units ordinarily do their monthly inactive duty training (IDT) drills on location with their SMCR command. They are integral to the unit and are expected to mobilize and operate with their assigned unit.
- *Individual augmentation units.* Chaplain and RP billets are organized into Marine expeditionary force, religious (MEFREL) NR units that augment the T/O of Active Component Marine Corps commands. Reserve religious ministry personnel assigned to Active Component augmentation units are to be trained and supported as similarly as possible to their active duty counterparts. These NR units are composed entirely of chaplains and RPs, with a chaplain serving as the officer in charge (OIC). Personnel assigned to these units train to mission-essential task lists (METLs) established

by their respective Active Component commands in order to be ready for mobilization to their supported commands for major contingencies. Every effort should be made to facilitate frequent onsite IDT drills with the supported Active Component command in order to accommodate both Active and/or Reserve integration at the unit level. At a minimum, annual training with the supported command is required and expected. Coordination of onsite drills and ATs require close interface between the Active Component command chaplain of the supported command; the OIC of the supporting MEFREL; the Navy Operational Support Center (NOSC), where the MEFREL is located; Commander, Naval Reserve Forces Command (COMNAVRES-FORCOM) (N01G); and MARFORRES (REL).

Note: REL denotes an active duty, O-6 Navy chaplain.

Qualifications

Upon assignment to a USMC support billet and prior to mobilization, all Reserve Component chaplains and RPs must attain adequate training and experience that is commensurate with their position. Ordinarily, newly reported chaplains or RPs will use their first annual training period in the reporting year to attend Chaplain and Religious Program Specialist Expeditionary Skills Training (CREST). Religious program specialists must either hold the 2401 Navy enlisted classification (NEC) upon assignment to a billet or attain the NEC within one year of assignment. The 2401 NEC will be awarded to RPs upon successful completion of CREST. One additional year to attain the 2401 NEC may be granted to RPs who enlist under the advanced placement program or to chaplains who must complete the chaplain basic course in their first year of naval service. In any case, CREST must be completed successfully within a member's first two years of assignment. Waivers to the CREST requirement, based upon a member's previous qualifying military experience, will be considered on a case-by-case basis by the respective COMNAVRESFORCOM program manager.

In order to fulfill their responsibility as moral and ethical advisor to the commander, the supported command should ensure that the Reserve Component chaplains attend all schools (e.g., Naval Chaplains School, CREST) and advanced courses (e.g., Command and Staff College Distance Learning, annual Chaplain Corps Professional Development Training Course) that provide instruction in emerging Marine Corps religious ministry requirements across the range of military operations. When mobilization occurs, this prior training and experience ensures a swift and seamless transition by reservists to serve with Active Component Marine units. Chaplains and RPs must be prepared to mobilize to any environment, whether they are called to active duty with their own Marine Reserve unit or are required to fill vacancies in an active command's RMT.

Responsibilities

The COMNAVRESFORCOM (N01G) is responsible for detailing chaplains and RPs to valid billets. All senior grade chaplains (O-5 and O-6) and all MEFREL OICs are board-selected for billets via the annual National Command and Senior Officer (O5-O6)/Non-Command and Command Billet Screening and Assignment Board (APPLY).

Note: APPLY denotes that billets are available for junior officers to apply in order to promote and advance.

Officers in the grades of lieutenant commander and below are detailed to billets via the monthly junior officer on-line application process. Religious program specialists are detailed to billets by the COMNAVRESFORCOM RP program manager. Some inactive duty for training with travel (IDTT), additional training period (ATP), and active duty training (ADT) funding (see Categories of Reserve Training paragraph, page 2-7) is available to Reserve chaplains and RPs through their program manager.

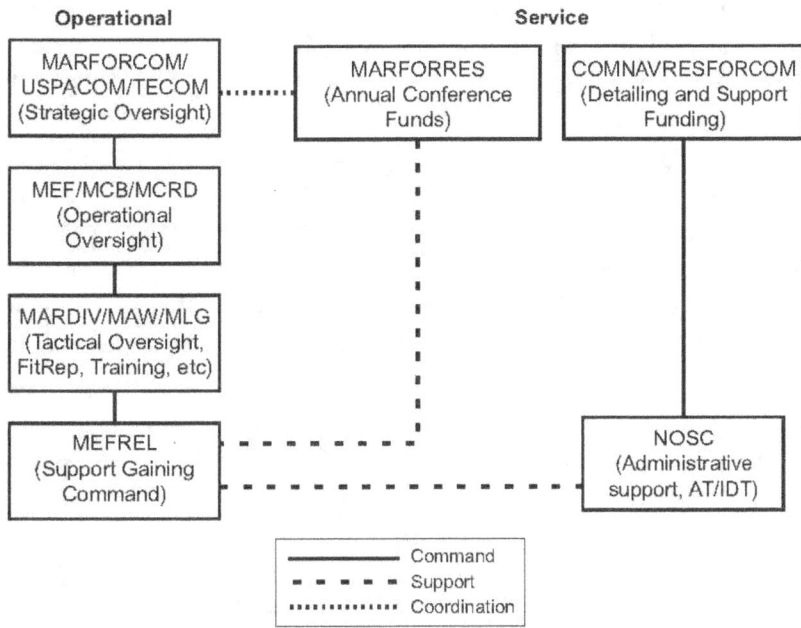

Figure 2-3. MEFREL Organizational Chart.

The NOSCs provide administrative support and IDT and annual training funding. All NR units have a designated supporting NOSC where participation is monitored and administrative and professional assistance is provided. Some IDTT, ATP, additional annual training, and/or ADT funding (see Categories of Reserve Training) may also be available through a supporting NOSC.

The MARFORRES (REL) provides strategic and operational oversight, as well as IDTT, ATP, and ADT funding (see Categories of Reserve Training) for all MARFORRES units and personnel. Some of these funds are also available for MEFREL chaplains and RPs in order to support on-site Reserve drilling with their supported command, other forms of training, and contributory support. The MARFORRES units issue field gear for practical training and supply organizational clothing for MARFORRES and MEFREL enlisted personnel.

Figure 2-3 describes how MEFREL units are aligned to Active Component operational units (MARDIV, MAW, and MLG). In addition, the MARFORCOM, MARFORPAC, and the Training and Education Command (TECOM) provide strategic oversight for their respective MEFRELs. The supported MEFs and MCBs of each MEFREL unit provide METLs and operational oversight. Both the Service component and operational units provide the necessary support and unit-specific training.

Categories of Reserve Training

The five categories of Reserve training are—

- *IDT.* Commonly referred to as a drill period, IDT is an authorized 4-hour period of training conducted to enhance the participating Navy Reservist's readiness for mobilization. The IDTs may be performed either with or without pay and may be performed at the local reserve center or other previously designated or authorized site.
- *IDTT.* This training category includes funds for the reservist to travel to a location other than the individual's normal drill site.

- *ATP.* The ATPs are extra, funded drill periods over-and-above the usual 48 annual drill periods. They are used for personnel matters, administrative matters, and some field evolutions.
- *Annual training.* Appropriated funds are used for annual training and scheduled through a NOSC for a minimum of 12 days active duty and one day of travel. A maximum of 17 days and 2 days of travel may be authorized for Marine Corps support, especially if travel outside the continental United States (OCONUS) is involved. The annual training of 12 days duration is the minimum period of active duty training or participation that Selected Reserve members must perform each year to satisfy training requirements and receive a satisfactory year for retirement. It is used for contributory support of a gaining command's mission and/or for training and attending Service schools, with the exception of CREST, which requires a longer period of time. The first annual active duty period must be attendance at CREST to ensure competency of follow-on contributory support. After completion of CREST, subsequent ATPs and drills are performed at the supported command.
- *ADT.* The funding for ADT is available for additional active duty days for Reserve Component members. There are particular ADT funds (e.g., ADT schools) that are set aside each year for Reservists training in Navy schools, including CREST.

Nonpay additional drills may be performed by the Reservist to earn one retirement point a day for a 4-hour drill. There are no limits to the amount of nonpay drill days, but only 90 total drills will be credited in any retirement year.

For additional information regarding annual training, ADT, IDT, IDTT, ATP, and Reserve drills, refer to the Bureau of Naval Personnel Instruction (BUPERSINST) 1001.39_, *Administrative Procedures for Navy Reservists on Inactive Duty.*

Operational Support

The active duty for special work (ADSW) program supports short-term mission requirements for which no permanent duty billet or position is programmed or where Active Component personnel with the required skills are unavailable. The ADSW program is not for training and not designed to fill gapped Active Component billets. Commands requiring long-term solutions should consider general recalls and/or mobilization. Typically, ADSW is 90 to 179 days in duration, to include recall and separation processing of members. Prior to orders being issued, applicants must be a satisfactory performer in the Selected Reserve or a VTU and meet the minimum additional requirements spelled out in the Chief of Naval Operations Instruction (OPNAVINST) 1001.20_, *Standardized Policy and Procedures for the Active Duty for Special Work (ADSW) and One Year Recall (OYR) Program.*

Mobilization Process

When personnel requirements for military operations exceed the shape or availability of the Active Component T/O, the appropriate Marine Corps component commander may determine to mobilize MARFORRES commissioned units that include RMTs and/or to augment Active Component religious ministry capabilities with individual augmentation personnel. For IA personnel, Active Component MEFs and MARFORs must look to their respective Reserve Component MEFREL unit(s) for personnel assets and collaborate with MARFORRES as requirements are developed. Orders may be issued to a reservist on the unit T/O for 365 days for forward deployment OCONUS. The rotation is determined by the Active Component unit. See 19 January 2007 Secretary of Defense Memorandum, *Utilization of the Total Force* and Naval Military Personnel Manual (NAVPERS) 15560D, *Naval Military Personnel Manual (MILPERSMAN),* article 1050-272 (Post-Mobilization Respite Absence for Mobilized Reserve Component Personnel).

When an RMT member returns from either Operation Iraqi Freedom (OIF) or Operation Enduring Freedom (OEF), the current policy prescribes that he may not be involuntarily mobilized for a period 5 times the length of his mobilization (i.e., 1:5 ratio of time between deployments). Voluntary mobilization can occur at any time. The Reserve Mobilization and Sailor Advocacy Team, which is located at the Navy Personnel Command in Millington, TN [NESA@navy.mil<mailto:NESA@navy.mil] is available to answer questions with any issues on mobilization for Operations OEF/Noble Eagle.

In the case of mobilization of an RMT prior to the RP attaining the required NEC, the RP may be mobilized to CREST with follow-on orders to active duty within a year. Total active service time, including CREST, cannot exceed the authority of the Presidential Executive Order 13223, of September 14, 2001: "Additional authority [for this mobilization is afforded] under [United States Code, Title 10:] to order any unit, and any member of the Ready Reserve not assigned to a unit organized to serve as a unit, to active duty for not more than 24 consecutive months."

Reserve members may be mobilized for greater than 365 days if command employment is still valid and the member agrees in writing by signing a Noble Eagle Sailor Advocacy (NESA) agreement. The command may send the member on temporary additional duty to another requirement if the original requirement is no longer valid. A member may also be reassigned to a different mobilization requirement. Additional days of post-mobilization respite absence will accrue (see MILPERSMAN article 1050-272). See appendix B for the current process for mobilization. For joint doctrine instruction on the mobilization process, see Joint Publication (JP) 4-05, *Joint Mobilization Planning*.

Care of Reserve RMTs

Supervisory chaplains who obtain Reserve RMTs through one of the approved funding options (see chap. 4, page 4-4) must take appropriate steps to care for those serving in reservist status. Proper preparations for the arrival and utilization of Reservist RMTs will ensure that the following areas are adequately addressed:

- Supervisory chaplains must maximize MEFREL asset time at their supported command through use of annual training, ADT, and IDT funding and reimbursement of expenses by the supported command for lodging and mileage.
- The supported command should ensure that each Reserve chaplain and RP are supplied the required military equipment (the same standards as their Active Component counterparts) for the environment in which the unit will operate.
- Supervisory chaplains should communicate the value of the MEFREL RMT as an asset to the supported command. MEFREL RMTs are trained, available, and ready to support the command to which they are assigned. They can also receive valuable on the job training through the unit training program while on active duty supporting the command.
- Supervisory chaplains should learn and understand the administrative needs of the Reserve Component RMTs, including proper usage and preparation of fitness and evaluation reports and awards.
- Commands requesting the mobilization of Reserve RMTs should seek to understand the mobilization process and to mobilize Reserve RMTs only if absolutely necessary. Ordinarily, plans for mobilizations should be limited to a maximum period of 365 days per reservist. This time is inclusive of mobilization and/or demobilization processing, transportation, travel time, workups, days on location, and leave periods.

Religious Lay Leaders

The authority for lay leaders is granted in the MILPERSMAN paragraph 1730-010, Use of Lay Leaders in Religious Services. Both MCO 1730.6D and SECNAVINST 1730.7D state that commanders shall provide CRPs in support of religious requirements and preferences of authorized personnel. Lay leaders must have a written letter of recommendation or endorsement from their own religious organization. Commanders may appoint lay leaders to accommodate religious preferences and diversity in the command. Appointment of a lay leader responds to an identified requirement and will be in writing for a specified period, not to exceed one year. Only authorized personnel representing their own religious organization may be appointed. Commands shall appoint authorized personnel as lay leaders based on volunteerism, high moral character, motivation, religious interest, and certification by the appointee's religious organization. Commanders shall ensure that lay leaders are trained and supervised by a military chaplain. Religious program specialists shall not be assigned as lay leaders.

In supporting the religious requirements for which the lay leader has been appointed, he should first seek the services of a military chaplain or civilian RMP. When this is not possible or practical, he should seek to arrange transportation to an appropriate service in proximity of the command. Lacking these opportunities, the lay leader may provide a religious service for members of the lay leader's religious organization consistent with his lay status, and as authorized by his religious organization.

Lay-led religious services are integral to the CRP and subject to command supervision. In most cases, lay-led services constitute a temporary accommodation of specific religious requirements in an operational setting when the assigned chaplain is probably available, but not able to provide the specific service required by the specific religious requirement. Religious lay leader training is described in MCRP 6-12B, *Religious Lay Leaders Handbook*. Lay leader training programs do not diminish the command responsibility for verification of a lay leader's attitude, abilities, and in some cases, faith group certification, before appointment by the commander.

Temporary Employment of Civilian Religious Ministry Professionals

Under the criteria in the DODI 5010.37, *Efficiency Review, Position Management, and Resource Requirements Determination*, DON policy allows for the temporary employment of qualified civilian RMPs. This temporary employment is to meet requirements for delivering religious ministries to personnel of religious organizations when such requirements cannot be met by available Chaplain Corps officers or command-appointed lay leaders. Civilian RMPs shall be employed as contract RMPs to satisfy the needs of the CRP in the most economical and appropriate manner.

Contract RMPs must be endorsed by a religious organization as defined by the DOD in DODI 1304.28, *Guidance for the Appointment of Chaplains for the Military Departments*. Duties shall be religious and programmatic in nature, such as conducting religious services or providing religious education as required by the command.

Contract RMPs shall be contracted on a nonpersonal services basis using competitive procedures under the authority and regulations set forth in the Federal Acquisition Regulations, JP 4-0, *Doctrine for Logistic Support of Joint Operations*. Military personnel or civilian Government employees shall not supervise contractor personnel. In accordance with Federal Acquisition Regulations, commands shall assign a contracting officer's technical representative to monitor the contract RMP's performance. Contracts for RMPs shall not exceed one year. Contracts in support of the CRP are paid out of operation and maintenance (O&M) funds.

CHAPTER 3
RELIGIOUS MINISTRY PRINCIPLES FOR THE MARINE CORPS

The Mandate of Religious Ministry

Chaplains minister in the sea services to fulfill the spirit of the First Amendment to the US Constitution—to avoid the establishment of religion and to protect the free exercise of religious expression. While chaplains have many duties and responsibilities supporting the range of military operations, they also have the primary mandate to meet the religious, spiritual, moral, and ethical readiness needs of the people they are called to serve, and to function as a moral and ethical advisor to the command. In serving this primary objective, chaplains are required to professionally plan and execute a comprehensive CRP, which involves an integration of special staff officer and core chaplain capabilities as delineated in chapters 4 and 5.

Religious Organizational Endorsement and Command Religious Program Requirements

The chaplain is endorsed by his religious organization, which is the source of the chaplain's ecclesiastical credentials. Chaplains facilitate the needs of all faith groups, as well as providing for the needs of their own. The relationship the chaplain has with his religious organization is not separate from, but coexists with, the relationship to the Navy and Marine Corps. The conditions, standards, and context for ministry are determined by the naval service and the nature of military operations. Both the Navy and Marine Corps expect the chaplain to conduct ministry, not as an outsider visiting a military installation or participating in a military operation, but as a member of the command, with official duties and responsibilities. As commissioned officers and RMPs serving on the staff of the Marine commander, the chaplains will conduct the CRP according to the following guidelines:

- All provisions of pastoral ministry will be within the framework of the CRP.
- Pastoral ministry will be provided within the requirements, conditions, and standards of the Marine Corps.
- Pastoral ministry will be coordinated, and in cooperation with, the ministry of other chaplains; including those of other Military Services, contracted providers, and appointed lay leaders.
- All pastoral ministry will be designed to meet the religious needs of all members of the command, their family members, and other authorized personnel.

Mission-Essential Task List

Each unit commander will develop a METL as a tool for remaining focused on training and to ensure successful mission accomplishment. A METL contains the list of a command's essential tasks with appropriate conditions and performance standards and measures. The RMT must be aware of the METL as it relates to their function on a tactical, operational, or strategic level. The mission analysis and METL development processes are described in Marine Corps Warfighting Publication (MCWP) 5-1, *Marine Corps Planning Process*; MCRP 3-0A, *Unit Training Management Guide*; and Chairman of the Joint Chiefs of Staff Manual 3500.03B, *Joint Training Manual for the Armed Forces of the United States*.

The CCDR-generated joint mission-essential task list (JMETL) draws on the Universal Joint Task

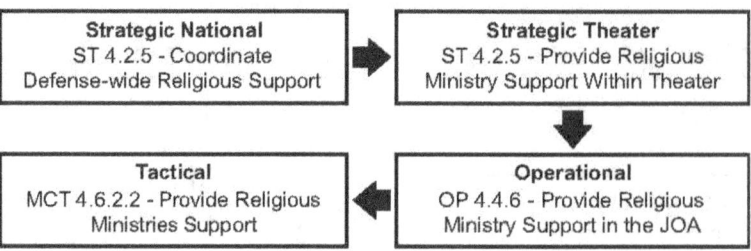

Figure 3-1. Levels of METs for the CRP.

List task library and lists the tasks, conditions, and standards that the CCDR identifies as required, assigned missions, which occur at the strategic level. Marine commanders at all levels employ a similarly disciplined process to review their mission assignments in a concept of operations, operation plan (OPLAN), operation order (OPORD), or other JMETL or METL from higher or adjacent units. A METL is a comprehensive command and mission-specific list of a unit's mission-essential tasks (METs). Generally, the RMT will have one MET with various tasks that support that MET. For example, the Universal Navy Task List as described in MCO 3500.26A, *Universal Naval Task List (UNTL)*, has levels of METs for the CRP at the strategic national, strategic theater, operational, and tactical levels (see fig. 3-1.). Each of these METs has standards and measures to ensure that the task is being conducted to support the MET.

The Marine Corps task list (MCTL), chapter 4 of MCO 3500.26A, states one MET of the RMT's is to provide religious support to components of the MAGTF (MCT [Marine Corps Tactical Task] 4.6.2.2, *Provide Religious Ministries Support*). Religious ministry teams perform ecclesiastical functions and provide coaching, counseling, and guidance for all personnel. This support serves to promote the spiritual, religious, ethical, moral, corporate, and personal well-being of Marines, Sailors, and their family members; thereby, enhancing personal, family, and unit readiness of the Marine Corps.

Table 3-1 shows 4 of the 20 total standards and measures (M1-M4) from the MCTL that the commander will enlist to assist him in—

- Completing the primary mission to provide religious ministries support to personnel within the components of the MAGTF.
- Establishing and coordinating a MAGTF religious ministry plan that will provide chaplain coverage to all elements.

The M1-M4 are measurements for determining if this MET is being completed and the CRP is mission capable.

Table 3-1. Example of METs.

Standard	Measurement and Description
M1	Percent of deviation from criteria for assignment of RPs and/or CAs.
M2	Percent of major military locations with services for all major denominations available on weekly basis.
M3	Percent of authorized chaplains assigned and present for duty.
M4	Percent of chaplains' time spent with military personnel in work areas.
Percentage will be determined by each category of standards of readiness for a particular unit.	

Defense Readiness Reporting System

Mission readiness is reported according to the command's METL using the newly developed Enhanced Status of Resources and Training System (ESORTS) software. The ESORTS database is being populated with existing tasks found in the Universal Joint Task List as well as the current version of Service task lists. By ensuring that the current version of the MCTL is revised and approved, the ESORTS database can be populated with applicable and accurate Marine Corps tasks for use by operational units to comply with the Defense Readiness Reporting System (DRRS) requirements.

It is important that RMTs at each of the three levels—strategic, operational, and tactical—understand that standards and measures is a form of Status of Resources and Training System (SORTS) reporting. The DRRS is updated monthly from very broad and specific tasks that flow from the battalion level, to the MARFORs, to the CCDR, so the RMT may make an informed decision on many areas within the command. Not all commands will be required to provide information on the readiness of RMTs. This will be tied to the mission of the command and its level.

Religious Ministry Principles

While the mandate of religious ministry in the Marine Corps is rooted in the free exercise of religion in an institutional setting with reporting and readiness requirements, there are other significant principles of ministry that are essential for a comprehensive CRP that meets the religious, spiritual, moral, and ethical readiness needs of Service members. These principles include guiding and operational principles. It is the dynamic faith and personal integrity of the chaplains serving the men and women of the Marine Corps that will bring these principles to life.

Guiding Principles

As an organization comprised of individuals called to serve our Sailors, Marines, and their families, the Chaplain Corps' guiding principles reflect a commitment and dedication to DON Core Values. Marine Corps CRPs should continually be evaluated to ensure that they are implemented in accordance with the following guiding principles:

- Promote the spiritual well-being of Sailors, Marines, and their families, in accordance with the first amendment, by respecting and accommodating their diverse religious requirements:
  - Administer CRPs that are comprehensive and support the free exercise of religion, while simultaneously honoring the Constitutional provision of nonestablishment.
  - Provide and accurately publicize divine services, with each chaplain serving according to the manner and forms of his religious organization.
  - Perform professional duties in cooperation with chaplains and civilian RMPs from other religious traditions.
  - Recognize that our diversity within the Chaplain Corps is a strategic organizational strength and signals that the Navy and Marine Corps welcome the service of persons of diverse backgrounds.
- Demonstrate spiritual and moral integrity:
  - Hold one another to the highest standards of moral and ethical behavior.
  - Protect confidential communications, honoring the sacred trust placed upon chaplains by those whom they serve.
  - Offer informed and objective advice, both up and down the chain of command.
  - Exercise supervisory responsibilities with the utmost commitment to the professional and personal development of subordinates.
- Model and teach that every person should be treated with human dignity:
  - Value, understand, and respect differences in gender, culture, race, ethnicity, and religion.

- ◆ Promote communication and conflict resolution skills to build strong relationships with Service members, family members, and communities with whom the Navy and Marine Corps interact throughout the world.
- Project professionalism and accountability:
  - ◆ Identify required capabilities and equip chaplains and RPs with the requisite competencies for success.
  - ◆ Develop, implement, and monitor policies, doctrine, measures of performance, and measures of effectiveness.
  - ◆ Implement both continuous planning and improvement processes in order to project and plan for current, near-term, and long-term religious requirements.

Operational Principles

Responsive Religious Ministry

Religious ministry at all levels should be simultaneously responsive to both the commander's METs and the individual religious needs of the Marines and Sailors. In the case of operational religious ministry based on the command's METs, special attention must be paid to ensure that it is appropriate to the command's mission, location, alert status, operating environment and tempo, current threat, and other conditions that affect ministry requirements. Since real world events or political decisions may change these conditions in a matter of hours, flexibility remains essential. Religious ministry support for operations is explained in greater detail in chapter 6.

Ministry of Purpose

Operational religious ministry flows from an expeditionary mindset. Time, personnel, and the limited resources of expeditionary forces demand purposeful actions at every level. Ministry is not only responsive, but must also be intentional and proactive.

Consequently, RMT actions should also be purposeful and intentional. Decisions concerning what ministry is appropriate must reflect consideration of the unintended consequences, as well as the immediate need. During any operation or exercise, the "right" ministry will meet the greatest need while supporting the primary mission of the command. Ministry, in any form, should neither interfere with the mission nor cause the RMT to become a liability to the unit. In the fluidity of military operations, the focus of effort for the RMT must match the focus of effort for the unit.

A ministry of purpose extends beyond a "ministry of presence." The RMT with a plan of action that has been well thought out prior to an operation or exercise will be more effective (see app. C).

Mission and Focus of Effort

The mission of RMTs in every military operation is to provide and facilitate appropriate ministries that support the religious needs and preferences of all members of the force or command. In times of crisis, such religious ministries are the core of the RMT's role in support of the commander's mission and the force's operational readiness. Careful RMT preparation requires attention to the various anticipated circumstances and the options of ministry to meet those circumstances. While an RMT's efforts may be focused on one of these options, sudden events may immediately change the team's focus of effort (e.g., mass casualties, emergent traumatic reactions).

There will also be times of temporary change of focus, which require discernment in the application of effort. For example, the demand for religious accommodations for faith groups with specific seasonal needs requires extra effort to arrange for visits from RMPs not attached to the command. However, while operations involving misplaced persons, evacuees, and even detained personnel may seem to commanders to be appropriate missions for RMTs, care should be taken to ensure RMT employment is never in conflict with their primary mission. Proper understanding of the mission of the command, needs of attached command personnel for religious ministry, and availability of chaplain and RMP inventory can allow for advance planning to meet these command and personnel needs.

Planning

MCDP 5, *Planning*, identifies five key functions of planning and plans. These concepts are central to the Marine Corps Planning Process and to the development and implementation of a comprehensive religious ministry plan for any operation. As with all aspects of military operations, effective religious ministry begins with planning and predeployment actions. Every aspect of the religious ministry Planning, Programming, Budgeting, and Execution process is focused on providing an innovative and comprehensive CRP for Marines, Sailors, authorized personnel, and their families.

Whether deployed, preparing for deployment, or redeployed, Marines, Sailors and their families are entitled to deliberate, well-executed religious programs that focus on their needs and requirements. An awareness of the Marine Corps Planning Process will serve RMTs well in developing and practicing sound religious ministry principles. The following five functions demonstrate the importance of understanding the commander's intentions when developing plans.

The first key function in planning is to "... direct and coordinate action by instructing those within the unit what to do and informing those outside the unit how to cooperate and provide support." (MCDP 5) Effective ministry is both proactive and responsive. Awareness of the commander's intentions will help the RMTs anticipate the fundamental requirements for ministry during the planning of an operation or exercise. This allows for intentional preparation and coordination of effort. As with any operation's planning, RMTs must consider external, internal, and task-related factors when planning and coordinating operational religious ministry. Such factors include a clear understanding of the mission and the commander's intent; a comprehensive analysis of

local religions; and the impact of religious customs, traditions, and culture on the mission and vice-versa. Timely and accurate RMT input to the command's deliberate planning process is essential for the development of the operational religious ministry section of the commander's estimates in both the OPORD and OPLAN.

Secondly, "planning develops a shared situational awareness." (MCDP 5) The commander's intent is based on the intelligence and research of his staff, and it informs the RMT of the environment in which religious ministry will be conducted. Awareness of the threat level, local cooperation possibilities, and requirements for travel in theater will prepare the RMTs to minister more effectively.

The impact that culture and religion may have on the mission will depend largely on the role religion plays in the daily life of opposing force and indigenous population (e.g., daily prayers may be a requirement for practicing members of a particular faith). RMTs may need to advise commanders that certain activities or behavior may be perceived as inflammatory by members of the opposing force and/or indigenous persons, causing unintended consequences. Situational awareness includes attention to all factors that impact individual and unit readiness. When Marines are unprepared physically, emotionally, intellectually, morally, or spiritually, they may have difficulty focusing on the mission. In times of stress or crisis, overlooking basic religious needs (i.e., required sacramental or ritual observances) and essential faith practices may have a negative ipact on personal readiness and unit morale.

The third key function demands that "planning generates expectations about how actions will evolve and how they will affect the desired outcome." (MCDP 5) Religious ministry during operations focuses on essentials. Much of the RMT's ministry to command members takes place as they prepare for operations. By proactively planning and providing for the religious requirements of the force, RMTs ensure effective response to emerging religious ministry needs (e.g., ministry to the wounded and dying, assistance with evacuations). Commanders expect their RMTs to be accessible and ready to respond. The RMTs are uniquely prepared for a critical role that centers on nurturing the living, caring for the sick or wounded, and honoring the dead.

"Planning supports the exercise of initiative" (MCDP 5) as the fourth key function. Solid planning facilitates timely response to changing events. Deficiencies are easier to detect, and options departing from the plan can be better identified and generated. The RMTs are trained to adapt ministry to the changing environment and emerging needs. While force planning for religious ministry is done at the MSC level and higher, all levels of command include operational planning for religious ministry. By being involved in planning an operation, the RMT can better anticipate where the need will be. If unforeseen needs arise, the RMT can respond in accordance with the intent of the plan (e.g., where and when to administer sacraments, prayers, and ministry to the wounded and dying).

The final, and fifth, key function requires "planning [to shape] the thinking of planners." (MCDP 5) Planning provides a disciplined framework for approaching problems. The experience of developing a plan can make an RMT more responsive to changing circumstances. The RMTs must take into consideration how their actions will affect the readiness and effectiveness of the Marines and Sailors to whom they minister. Additionally, they must maintain situational awareness, providing ministry at the appropriate time. When, in the course of an operation, religious ministry plans are overcome by events, RMTs must adapt and move on. Ministry to people must never be allowed to jeopardize the security of those to whom the ministry is being provided.

There will be times when RMTs must react rather than plan to respond. That does not relieve RMTs from the responsibility of planning. Planning helps ensure that one's reaction to the unexpected is the appropriate response. It is through planning, testing, and *replanning* that chaplains and RPs develop their ability to respond appropriately.

The Marine Corps Planning Process is a six-step methodology that helps organize the thought processes of the commander and staff throughout the planning and execution of military operations (see fig. 3-2). This process focuses on the mission and the threat and is based upon the Marine Corps' philosophy of maneuver warfare and the doctrine set forth in MCDP 5. It capitalizes on the principle of unity of effort and supports the establishment and maintenance of tempo.

The first step in the planning process is mission analysis. The commander's intentions can be found in the OPORD. The force chaplain will write Appendix 6 (Chaplain Activities) to Annex E (Personnel) of the OPORD, expressing how the commander expects religious ministry to be deployed. The commander's intentions are combined with all other research into the anticipated mission and become the foundation for the Marine Corps Planning Process. Awareness of these factors also becomes a part of RMT mission analysis, along with other information gathered on the geography, culture, infrastructure, force locations, and employment. The analysis of the mission is fundamental to intentional RMT planning. Reading the OPORD and conducting the research are necessary prior to planning.

The next step in the planning process is the development of all reasonable and possible courses of action (COAs). The COAs are designed so they may be wargamed and/or practiced. The RMT's awareness of, and involvement in, the development of various COAs enables planning of religious ministry to meet each circumstance.

Developed COAs are simulated into war games to better identify benefits and risks. The RMTs can also creatively imagine their own responses to various COAs deployed and enacted in order to identify the efficacy of their plans.

During COA comparison and decision, benefits and risks are assessed and the COA is chosen. The chosen COA is put into action during step 5, orders development. For RMTs emulating this process, the chosen COA becomes the focus of their ministry plans.

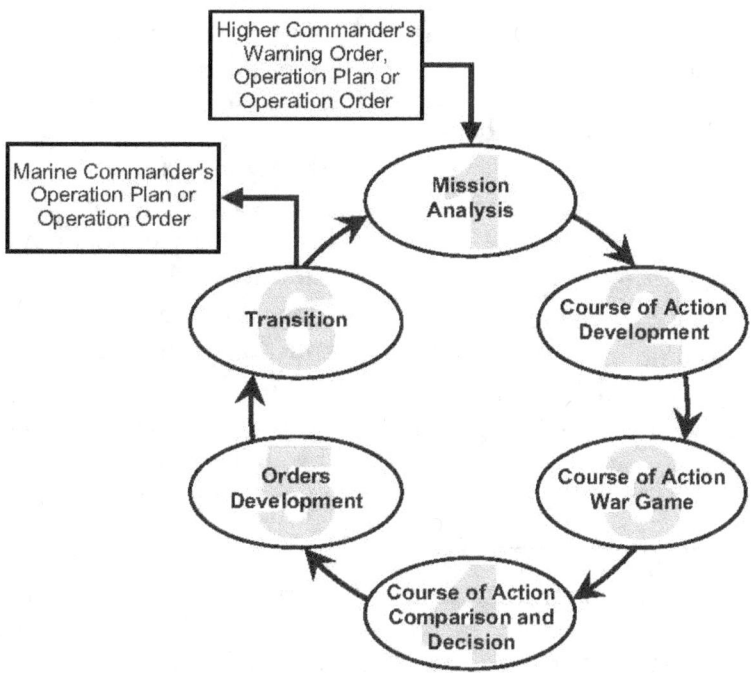

Figure 3-2. Marine Corps Planning Process.

Step 6 addresses transition. The order is matched to the commander's intentions and becomes the OPLAN or OPORD. This step also leads back to mission analysis as an ongoing process, reminding RMTs that plans must remain responsive to a changing environment.

There are several pitfalls to planning for religious ministry, especially in an expeditionary environment. Awareness of the following common mistakes will assist RMTs in guarding against these pitfalls:

- Attempting to forecast and dictate events too far into the future (e.g., planning worship services to Marines and Sailors dispersed in the field prior to obtaining exact unit locations can result in poor planning for ground transportation to dispersed units; whereas, awareness of COAs can prevent these errors).

- Trying to plan in too much detail (e.g., attempting to construct community relations [COMREL] projects prior to meeting local host nation leaders).

- Using planning as a scripting process that tries to prescribe friendly and possibly enemy actions with precision (e.g., assuming that tactical operations will place a unit in a precise location after the completion of the mission; not attending OPORD meetings to understand and anticipate ministry needs of upcoming operations).

- Adapting institutionalized planning methods that lead to inflexible thinking and rigid procedures (e.g., limiting use of resources to what is immediately available).

Mutual Support

Through mutual support, RMTs provide a broad, comprehensive religious ministry to their assigned commands and enhance the CRPs of other commands. Mutual support requires coordination between units, and in some cases, between Services. This will require a thorough and accurate understanding of the chain of command and the commander's intent to accommodate mutual support of other units' personnel. This is true for both supported and supporting commands. When the commander's intent is to provide mutual support to other units or Services, some guiding principles apply. Chaplains will—

- Facilitate religious ministry for members of other faith groups.
- Provide specific religious ministries to members of their own faith.
- Deliver pastoral care to all military members, their families, and authorized personnel.
- Advise the command on the impact of religion and the CRP on the command, as well as the impact of religion on the command's external mission.

Confidential Communication

Confidentiality is the cornerstone of pastoral care for Navy chaplains. The unconstrained ability to discuss personal matters in complete privacy encourages personnel and family members seeking chaplain assistance to speak freely, without fear of recrimination in pursuing their need for pastoral care. Such ability to speak freely establishes a sacred trust, facilitates increased morale and mission readiness, and benefits both the individual and the institution. Confidential communication includes acts of religion, matters of conscience, and any other information conveyed to a chaplain. Confidential communication may be conveyed through oral or written means, including electronically. All chaplains have the professional obligation to maintain the privacy of all confidential communication disclosed to them in their official capacities. All RPs and Marine CAs working for chaplains are also required to maintain confidential communication relationships. This is true, either if they inadvertently overhear such communication or if a member discloses information to them in their role as an RP or Marine CA.

Other members of the RMT, such as lay leaders and other support personnel in the CRP, are not covered by the provisions of being recipients of confidential communications; but are bound to maintain such confidences if they inadvertently overhear or discover them.

The term "confidential communications" includes the legal recognition of the clergy-penitent privilege, all communication between Navy chaplains and those who confide in them as an act of religion, a matter of conscience, or in their role as spiritual advisors. This is considered a right for those who seek out chaplains for this purpose. Commanders and chaplains are required to honor the confidential relationship between Service personnel and military chaplains.

Privileged communication is a subset of confidentiality and may also be known as "religious privilege," "priest-penitent privilege," or "clergy privilege." The *United States Manual of Courts-Martial,* Military Rules of Evidence 503, *Communications to Clergy,* defines the chaplain-penitent privilege for military chaplains and Service members. This evidentiary rule recognizes that certain communications to clergy should be held confidential as a matter of public policy and outweighs the Government's interest in securing a criminal prosecution. The chaplain, the penitent, and even certain third parties present during the communication cannot be compelled to disclose qualifying communications. "Privilege" is applied when a communication is made to a chaplain in his capacity as a spiritual advisor or to a CA acting in an official capacity. The official policy is detailed in SECNAVINST 1730.9.

Various conferences and boards relating to military chaplaincy have contributed to current understandings and applications of important concerns with regard to confidentiality. The unofficial code of ethics cited in chapter 1 contains the following statement on confidentiality:

> *I will hold in confidence any privileged communication received by me during the conduct of my ministry. I will not disclose confidential communications in private or public.*

The RMT acts as a shoreline of safety, toward which the spiritually stressed and those seeking wisdom search for clarity, guidance, and healing. Concerning the duty of leading Marines and Sailors to healing, RMTs must be confident in both their understanding of the sacred trust that constitutes the basis of their ministry and in their ability to work within the active silence of confidentiality and privilege.

Pastoral/Professional Care Network

Chaplains maintain professional relationships with other care providers and agencies within the military and civilian communities. Referrals often enable RMTs to provide the type of professional support required by Service members and their families. Direct support organizations—the American Red Cross (ARC), Navy-Marine Corps Relief Society, MCCS/Fleet and Family Support Centers, and the Salvation Army—provide a wide range of professional services. RMTs should constantly update their working database of professional services in their geographic operational area.

Religious ministry teams maintain working relationships with legal assistance offices, family readiness officers (FROs), MCCS, hospitals, alcohol and drug rehabilitation centers, and other military and civilian resources. Similarly, RMTs maintaining their professional relationships with local community religious organizations enable appropriate referrals for specific religious requirements and needs.

Marine Corps Family Team Building and Other Supported Programs

Marine Corps Family Team Building (MCFTB) is a major program involved in enhancing family readiness. The MCO 1754.6A, *Marine Corps Family Team Building (MCFTB)*, describes family readiness as "families who are prepared and

equipped with the skills and tools necessary to successfully meet the challenges of the military lifestyle." Given their professional training, position, and role in the command, chaplains are active contributors to the MCFTB program, and they are a natural bridge between families and the chain of command.

Personal and family readiness staff personnel provide required direct support for the maintenance and operation of the MCFTB programs, which include KVN; Lifestyles, Insights, Networking, Knowledge, and Skills (L.I.N.K.S.); Spouses' Learning Series; CREDO; and Prevention and Relationship Enhancement Programs (PREP).

Increasingly, *family* readiness is viewed as a key factor in overall unit readiness. Family issues, if not addressed, can have a significant impact on unit readiness and cohesiveness. The Marine Corps family readiness programs instituted in recent years are designed to provide a support mechanism to help address family concerns. Collectively, these programs support optimum unit effectiveness and mission readiness, prepare Marine families to meet the challenges of the military lifestyle, and standardize the policies and functions of the MCFTB programs across organizations and duty stations.

A significant number of observations and lessons learned from operations in the United States Marine Corps Central Command's operational area (available on the Marine Corps Center for Lessons Learned [MCCLL] Web site) have provided insight into the strengths of the MCFTB and its component programs, as well as identifying areas for improvement.

Family Readiness Officers

The MCO 1754.6A prohibits chaplains from serving as FROs. Chaplains need to be available to deploy with their unit while other qualified personnel fulfill the role of the FRO. Chaplains must maintain a close working relationship with FROs.

The FROs are vital to the life and health of a deployed unit. The FRO should ensure that the state of family readiness is constantly promoted through a well-planned and carefully executed program for his assigned unit(s). These units include those traditionally referred to as "non-deploying" units, as well as deploying units.

Family members of all units have to be prepared for separations. When a Marine or Sailor deploys, the deployment cycle is a major event in the lives of family members. Clear and direct communication is the most effective means of limiting the stress of a deployment. The unit's leadership and demonstrated concern for families during all phases of deployment directly affects the success of the unit's family readiness efforts. The FRO communicates the commander's goals and vision for family readiness; information about the unit's mission; and how to link unit members, family members, MCCS, and community resources. For more information on the FRO program, see Navy/Marine Corps Directive (NAVMC DIR) 1754.6A, *Marine Corps Family Team Building (MCFTB)*, and Marine Corps Bulletin (MCBul) 1754, *Primary Duty Family Readiness Officers (FROs)*.

Marine Corps Mentoring Program

Chaplains are cited in NAVMC DIR 1500.58, *Marine Corps Mentoring Program (MCMP) Guidebook,* as a resource for Marines who need assistance with spiritual guidance, stress management, combat and operational stress care, and individual encouragement and general support. Chaplains are highly encouraged to take a proactive role in assisting in the ethical and moral development and growth of Marines and Sailors assigned to their care, by partnering with senior enlisted and officers within their unit in implementing this program. Additional information may be found in NAVMC DIR 1500.58 and MCO 1500.58, *Marine Corps Mentoring Program.*

Family Advocacy Program

Chaplains play a critical role as a community responder (e.g., medical, legal, base security and law enforcement, educators, counselors, advocates, chaplains) in the Family Advocacy Program (FAP). They should be trained in identifying family violence risk factors and dynamics, basic community information and referral, safety planning, and appropriate responses as a professional—to include screening procedures, identification, assessment, and sensitive interviewing of victims. The FAP manager responsible for the FAP local program is responsible for providing this training. While chaplains are not prohibited from attending the FAP case review committee during risk assessment and treatment planning deliberations, they are not designated as permanent voting members during the incident status determination phase. Chaplains should not serve as case review committee voting members. More specific program guidance may be found in SECNAVINST 1752.3B, *Family Advocacy Program (FAP).*

Sexual Assault Prevention and Response Program

All chaplains are expected to receive the periodic training in sexual assault prevention and response (SAPR) per SECNAVINST 1752.4A, *Sexual Assault Prevention and Response,* and MCO 1752.5A, *Sexual Assault Prevention and Response Program.* Chaplains play an integral role in SAPR along with Marine and Family Services personnel (i.e., counselors and victim advocates) and health care professionals.

Exceptional Family Member Program

The Exceptional Family Member (EFM) Program includes the identification, enrollment, and tracking of all eligible family members with special medical and educational needs, regardless of where the sponsor is assigned. This program is detailed in SECNAVINST 1754.5B, *Exceptional Family Member Program.*

Marine for Life Program

The Marine for Life (M4L) Program is designed to expand transition assistance and provide sponsorship for the more than 27,000 Marines who honorably leave active service each year and return to civilian life. The M4L Program formally extends our commitment to take care of our own and nurtures mutually beneficial relationships inherent in our ethos—once a Marine, always a Marine. The MCO 1754.8A, *Marine for Life (M4L) Program*, directs the program.

Self-Care

A critical principle of religious ministry is the care of the deliverer. While RMTs specialize in taking care of other people, they are frequently not as good at taking care of themselves. With this in mind, the importance of RMT self-care cannot be overstated. Chaplains and RPs are at risk for fatigue and stress because of their unique role as caregivers. A continuous practice of basic physical, psychosocial, intellectual, and spiritual disciplines keep the RMT healthy and conditioned to care for others (see fig. 3-3 on page 3-12).

The RMTs offer a link to both the spiritual and the divine. They are the only personnel in the command officially designed by MOS and policy to claim this professional territory. The RMTs are the gatekeepers, or "lane" keepers, of the innovative delivery of religious ministry and compassionate pastoral care. Lack of self-care causes one to run out of resources to help others. Additionally, the RMT sets a poor example for others.

Physical

Physical self-care is the most immediately observable sign of wholeness or brokenness in a person. Regular attention to physical training, as well as good general medical care, are important ways for RMTs to take care of themselves. A well-conditioned RMT is better able to withstand the stressors of the day-to-day demands of the CRP.

Modeling good physical health through proper rest, exercising, consuming a healthy diet, and avoiding abuse of substances pays dividends individually for the RMT and collectively for the unit.

Psychosocial

The emotional health of RMTs impacts directly on their ability to provide religious ministry. Understanding and managing emotions can minimize the negative effects of stress and help build strong, appropriate relationships with family, friends, colleagues, mentors, communities of faith, and the recipients of ministry.

Seeking psychological self-awareness can bring healing and growth. Learning to manage emotional stress and how to deal effectively with conflict can reduce relational and personal difficulties. Support from colleagues and mentors can sustain personal and professional development. Finally, the ability to enjoy life through play and recreation contributes to a resilient personality that retains the capacity for joy. These practices add to a psychosocial well-being and the balance of a whole being, enabling better care to others.

Intellectual

Intellectual growth is both a personal wholeness, as well as a professional competence issue. Chaplains and RPs are required to receive advanced and refresher training on a regular basis, as directed by higher authority. Examples of this training include Chaplain Corps Professional Development Training Workshops (PDTWs) and Professional Development Training Courses (PDTCs), joint professional military education, the Doctor of Ministry Program, postgraduate education, clinical pastoral education, local area training events, denominational training oppor-tunities, and self-directed study and reading. Taking the time to pursue these programs during busy schedules, though challenging, should be a priority of the RMT. Good intellectual health is as important for the growth and sustenance of RMTs as is physical training. Sustaining intellectual and professional competencies not only serves the RMT well, but also the unit and future units of that RMT. Senior and supervisory RMTs should promote and make

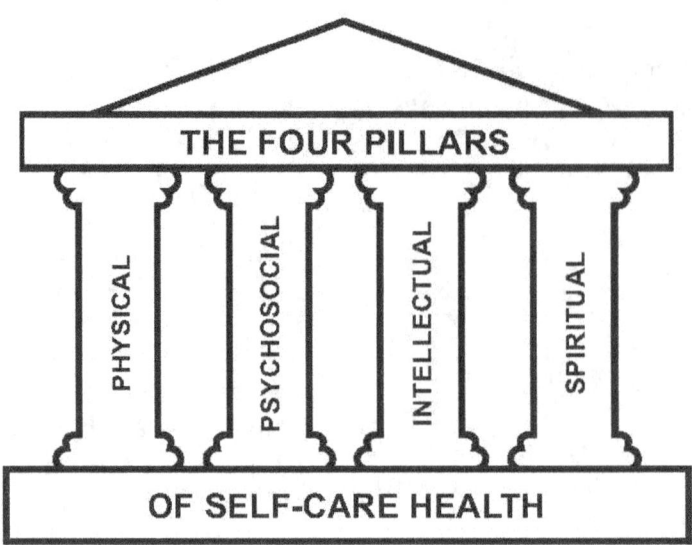

Figure 3-3. The Four Pillars of Self-Care Health.

time for junior RMTs to pursue a broad range of intellectually and professionally rewarding training and study.

Spiritual

The RMT holds a unique position in the command to facilitate spiritual health and healing in Marines and Sailors. Neglecting spiritual self-care can negatively impact the ability of the RMT to carry out their higher calling to connect Marines and Sailors to spiritual sources.

Spirituality is the expression of the human spiritual nature in thoughts, actions, and relationships. Being disciplined in the growth of personal spiritual understanding, personal spiritual disciplines, and personal spiritual connections with others and the divine causes chaplains and RPs to grow personally and replenish their resources for caring for others. Intentional practices of study, prayer, worship, charity, service, silence, simplicity, and rest represent ways of invigorating spiritual health.

The RMTs are a symbol of hope, reminding each member of the command that they are not alone.

The RMTs are encouraged to attend CREDO retreats, to seek spiritual counsel from trusted advisors, and to continuously monitor and appraise their own spiritual focus and health in order to sustain their role as caregivers.

Buddy Care

Buddy care is integral to self-care. From the concept of battle buddies to the new emphasis on buddy care for caregivers, intentional actions of caring, trust, accountability, reciprocity, and follow-up are essential. Buddy care may involve checking on how another is doing, holding intentional sessions of goal setting and growth, or presenting direct debriefs of traumatic events. A key responsibility of buddies is to ensure buddies get the appropriate professional help when needed.

Group Care

The MAGTF chaplains can encourage and aid RMT self-care by offering Care for the Caregiver retreats. Chaplains in leadership positions, sometimes in cooperation with CREDO, MCFTB, or MCCS counseling offices may offer group settings for RMTs to process their deployment transition, both in-theater and postdeployment. Care for the Caregivers retreats have been held for RMTs alone and jointly with medical personnel.

Retreats can range from brainstorming and sharing sessions, to full multiday retreats with teaching, exercises, assignments, and goal setting. Some retreats have been held in-theater with fragmentary order (FRAGO) or chief of staff letter of instruction support. For example, a retreat may consist of large group brainstorming on simple questions, such as: How have you changed? What was good? What was bad? What do you need to do to readjust? These retreats are a time for RPs, chaplains, IAs, and Reserve RMTs to air their concerns, either separately or as a group. The more lengthy postdeployment retreats may include tools such as creative and expressive writing, trauma timelines, reflective time, and group sharing. Additional tools con-cerning group care are available through the Chaplain Corps PDTW sponsored by CREDO centers.

CHAPTER 4
STAFF OFFICER TASKS

Military Organization

Navy chaplains will be assigned as principal staff officers to assist commanders in the development, implementation, and support of religious ministries at each level of command. Chaplains advise commands in matters of morale, morals, ethics, and spiritual well-being. They also serve as advisors to commanders for the impact of religion on military operations. Chaplains are organizationally placed under the chief of staff or executive officer, while retaining direct access to the commanding officer in accordance with MCO 1730.6D.

As staff officers in a military organization, chaplains function according to the rules and regulations of the sea services. As commissioned officers, chaplains are subject to the Uniform Code of Military Justice (UCMJ) and are expected to observe good order and discipline.

A chaplain's belief system, concept of calling, and divine service does not diminish his responsibilities to fulfill the requirements of his commission.

Following orders and regulations, adhering to standing operating procedures (SOPs), fulfilling staff responsibilities to superiors and subordinates, and following the chain of command are not optional duties for chaplains. These duties are essential to successful institutional ministry and sound staff work. Furthermore, the institution values chaplains who show respect to the men and women they serve by becoming familiar with the dynamics of their environment.

Chaplains perform an important role because they can prophetically speak the truth in places and times where most Service members have little voice. An institutionally perceptive chaplain knows best when to speak the "truth to power" and how best to do so. Chaplains who are not aware of the system often miss opportunities to influence it, or sometimes find themselves in opposition to it, thus failing to be effective to the needs of their people. Knowing, practicing, and honing staff officer skills enhance the chaplain's credibility and value to the unit and the men and women they serve.

Officer Tasks

Chaplains must continuously seek to develop staff officer skills to be effective *institutional* ministers. Chaplains carry responsibilities identical to other officers: advising the commander; providing leadership, training, and education; and provisioning of resource management.

Advising the Commander

As staff officers, chaplains have the core capability task of advising commanders (see chap. 5, page 5-5).

Providing Leadership, Training, and Education

The chaplain will provide leadership, training, and education through appropriate professional military education (PME) and classes on topics such as ethics, character development, relational and life skills, personal and spiritual well-being, crisis and suicide awareness, domestic violence, grief and loss, values, cultural issues, and WT programs. Chaplains can also contribute to the moral and ethical leadership aspects of the Marine Corps Martial Arts Program.

Provisioning of Resource Management

The chaplain will contribute to the provisioning of resource management, which includes the proper leadership, management, supervision of people, administration of programs, and oversight of logistical needs of the CRP. As a staff officer for the Marine commander, the chaplain will address the specific areas, functions, and skill sets discussed in the following paragraphs.

Supervision, Leadership, and Management

Professional development of subordinates includes the supervision and measure of performance of all assigned personnel and volunteers. Senior chaplains within the command structure provide direct supervision of the CRP (e.g., a division chaplain, as the director for religious ministries on the staff of the division commander, oversees the CRP at all subordinate command levels). Senior chaplains also function as mentors for subordinate chaplains to adjust and adapt professionally to the unique military ministry setting. Marine commanders support a training program for chaplains, RPs, and Marine CAs assigned to their commands (see MCO P3500.44A, *Religious Ministry Team (RMT) Training & Readiness Manual*). Proper management of this program is under the cognizance of the senior supervisory chaplain to whom subordinate commands report.

CRP Inspections

Supervisory chaplains will ensure that an appropriate regimen of CRP inspections or assist visits are conducted at subordinate commands, deficiencies properly documented, and CRP personnel held accountable for performance and training in proper procedures.

Force Protection

While chaplains are noncombatants, all members of the CRP are responsible for practicing sound force protection practices. The antiterrorism awareness training Web site is a resource for force protection awareness and training. Additional information may be found in the SECNAVINST 3300.2B, *Department of the Navy (DON) Antiterrorism (AT) Program*.

Physical Fitness

Compliance with physical fitness and grooming standards is essential for RMTs serving with Marines. A rigorous physical fitness program ensures RMTs are fully capable of performing the demanding physical requirements associated with combat skills. As previously stated in the self-care paragraph in chapter 3, RMTs who practice a disciplined regimen of physical fitness are better physically qualified to do their jobs and gain the respect of Marines. For additional guidelines, see OPNAVINST 6110.1H w/ch 1, *Physical Readiness Program*.

Administration of Programs

The chaplain will assist and advise the commander in the administration of various programs as follows:

- *Fitness reports.* Preparing fitness reports and evaluations required for officers and enlisted members is a skill that must be learned and exercised to ensure the success of future RMTs. Supervisory chaplains will assist and advise unit commanders in preparation and appropriate submission of these reports per MCO 1730.6D. Further guidance on the preparation of reporting procedures is provided in BUPERSINST 1610.10A, *Navy Performance Evaluation System*.
- *Humanitarian transfers and conscientious objector.* Processing humanitarian transfers and conscientious objector assessments are essential staff officer tasks that are highly valued by the commander. Humanitarian transfer procedures are found in MILPERSMAN paragraph 1900-020, *Convenience of the Government Separation Based on Conscientious Objection (Enlisted and Officers)*, and NAVPERS 15909B, *Enlisted Transfer Manual*, for Navy personnel and in MCO P1000.6G, *Assignment, Classification, and Travel Systems Manual*, for Marine Corps

personnel. Conscientious objector interviews directed by the commanding officer are administrative functions and are not considered counseling relationships. They are not confidential communication and the chaplain shall inform the interviewee of this fact. If a chaplain has a prior counseling relationship with a Service member requesting designation as a conscientious objector, he shall not be appointed to evaluate that Service member for conscientious objector status, per MCO 1306.16E, *Conscientious Objectors*, and the command will appoint another chaplain to conduct the interview.

- *Equipment*. Preventive requirements must be performed on all equipment assigned to the RMT. This includes field gear and equipment used in support of religious worship.
- *Reporting requirements*. Monitor to ensure compliance with DRRS reporting protocols and all CRP and other inspection protocols. Ensure that subordinate command CRPs are reporting compliance data in the appropriate collection systems (DRRS and Chaplain Corps).
- *Performance*. A supervisor will measure performance by—
  - ◆ Collecting and analyzing data on subordinate units as required and reporting required information to higher headquarters.
  - ◆ Ensuring compliance with all recording and reporting protocols; inspection regimes; data collection, management, and reporting requirements; customer and command satisfaction surveys; and other data calls.
  - ◆ Monitoring the development and use of local CRP SOPs to delineate specific policies and responsibilities for the operation of the CRP, which will become the basis for reporting metrics.
  - ◆ Developing SOPs to define particular duties and functions of all members assigned to the CRP to include, at a minimum, program requirements and tasks, watch standing procedures, plans for response to disasters, support of the casualty assistance calls

officer (CACO) program, and coordination of area ministry. For further information on the CACO program, see NAVPERS Manual 15607C, *Casualty Assistance Calls Officer Handbook*, and MCO P3040.4E, *Marine Corps Casualty Procedures Manual*.

- ◆ Compiling periodic reports as required by the Chaplain of the Marine Corps, HQMC Code (REL), Information in these reports will include significant ministry accomplishments, data on the number of deployed RMTs, dwell time, and other emerging trends. This data is often used to establish and sustain manpower and funding requirements. Additionally, units deployed in a joint environment will have significant operational reporting requirements from higher headquarters as delineated in OPORDs.
- *After action reports and lessons learned*. Deployed RMTs and IAs are required to file after action reports (AARs) and/or lessons learned just prior to returning from deployments. These reports and lessons should be filed through/with the command lesson manager in the unit and submitted to the MCCLL, where reports of RMTs may be viewed on the Web site: https://www.mccll.usmc.mil/.

Logistics

The CRP is an official and integral part of each organization within the Marine Corps, as established by Title 10, United States Code, SECNAVINSTs, and Marine Corps directives. Each commander bears responsibility for logistical support for religious ministries. The commander's direct support of the religious ministry mission is contained in the MCO 1730.6D and states that, "Commanders will include the CRP as an integral and essential element of administration, planning, programming, and budgeting activities, supported with appropriated funds at a level consistent with other personnel programs within DON."

Logistical support of the RMT includes, but is not limited to, provision of adequate office space, furniture, equipment, supplies, support services, and transportation. Due to the sensitive nature of pastoral counseling and the professional study of chaplains, office spaces for chaplains should be accessible to Marines, Sailors, and their families, while providing sufficient privacy. A separate but adjunct administrative space for the chaplain's office is essential to accommodate the RP's administrative responsibilities and to provide an adequate waiting area. An office door with a window is required to eliminate perception of inappropriate activity by counselee or chaplain.

Logistical support for divine services, religious education, personal devotions, group activities, classes, and training require intentional planning and continual upkeep and maintenance. Transportation, radio communication (field and deployed), direct phone lines (garrison), adequate office furniture, up-to-date information technology, and connectivity are basic requirements to support comprehensive religious ministry.

Commands are accountable for all nonconsumable items. Unit commanders will ensure that a responsible officer (RO) from the CRP is assigned in writing. The RO will maintain an inventory of nonconsumable items purchased by O&M funds.

Appropriated Funds Management Principles

Religious ministry funding is derived from command-appropriated O&M funds and operates within the Planning, Programming, Budgeting, and Execution process. Adequate planning requires the inclusion of the religious ministry plan in the development of the command's budget. The command's design for ministry relies on the RMT's management of the following:

- *Budget and procurement resources.* The O&M funding, planning, programming, and budgeting will reflect current and anticipated program requirements that support the religious requirements of individuals and families served by the CRP. Commands will prepare and submit annual O&M budget estimates. When submitting CRP budgets, RMTs ensure that requirements are detailed, prioritized, and accurately estimated.

- *Needs assessment.* A comprehensive needs analysis/assessment is conducted to identify the command's religious ministry requirements of assigned personnel and establish the commander's priorities for religious ministry. This includes identifying specific faith groups represented within the command.

- *Mission and operational requirements.* There should be a thorough understanding of the command's mission and operational requirements.

- *Command's calendar.* The RMTs should have a working knowledge of the command's calendar for submission to the budget cycle.

- *Command's supply system.* There should be a functional understanding of the commands supply system and established working relationships with the supply department.

- *Command T/O.* There should be proper knowledge of the command T/O and utilization of Reserve assets. An active duty chaplain should plan for training Reserve assets assigned to the command and should budget accordingly to fund the travel and other expenses for the assigned Reservist's active duty training.

The following steps are crucial to the design of the CRP budget:

- *Plan the program.* Develop a comprehensive religious ministry plan based on the commander's priorities, identified needs, command mission, planned training and operations schedule, available assets, and possible contingencies.

- *Match the goals with the funds.* Translate the planned programs into dollar amounts.

- *Submit the plan.* The religious ministry plan should be submitted with the CRP budget for command approval and inclusion in the command's O&M funds.

- *Implement the funding.* Put the funded programs into operation.
- *Record the process.* Actual expenses and effective programs are documented to assist in future religious ministry plans and validating budget requirements.
- *Study the results.* By evaluating the effectiveness of the programs, the RMT develops a clear understanding of requirements and direction for future planning.

Nonappropriated Funds

The ROFs provide a vehicle for religious expression. Various religious traditions include the concept of voluntarily offering money and financial support of mission organizations as an aspect of religious life. Marines, Sailors, their family members, and authorized personnel are encouraged to express their religious devotion through direct stewardship and financial contributions to their faith groups and the CRP through the ROF. As a matter of policy, deployable commands neither establish nor maintain a ROF due to the inability to provide security and timely administration of the contributions. Contributions made within the context of worship in Marine Corps chapels are administered by the commanding officer or commander under the authority of SECNAVINST 7010.6A, *Religious Offering Fund,* and MCO 7010.17A, *Religious Offering Fund.* These formal instructions provide specific procedures for the administration of these nonappropriated funds.

Material Readiness and Accountability

Generally, the senior chaplain or the senior RP of the RMT is designated by the commander, in writing, as the RO for RMT equipment and assumes responsibility for the care, safekeeping, and maintenance of RMT property. This responsibility pertains to all Government property coming into his possession from any source, and by any means, until properly relieved. The signature of the designated RO on the proper documents is prima facie (at first sight) evidence that responsibility for the care and safekeeping of the public property has been accepted. A joint physical inventory is conducted annually-as directed by the commander, the RO, the individual holding the property accounts, or when the property is transferred to a newly designated RO.

Command Religious Program Tables of Equipment and Property Accounts

Marine commands and units maintain prescribed T/Es that include the essentials for religious ministry. The RMTs advise the commander and assist the supply officer to ensure the command or unit inventories include all authorized religious ministry T/E items. The RMTs generally maintain custody and ensure the religious ministry T/E items are properly maintained and ready for deployment. Periodic inspections and assist visits are conducted by the command or higher headquarters to evaluate command readiness, including the status of authorized T/E equipment and materials. Property, furniture, and equipment essential to religious ministry, but in addition to the T/E, are also controlled by the unit supply officer and are listed on the command property account. Subcustody (i.e., signed custody cards) and care of religious ministry equipment are generally assigned to the command's senior chaplain or RP.

Command Religious Program Facilities

Commanders may authorize use of chapels and religious support facilities for nonreligious meetings for any legitimate purpose. As Government property, religious support facilities are available for authorized purposes at no charge. Because chapels are provided for the free exercise of religion, religious services and activities for all recognized faith groups have first priority.

Chapels and religious support facilities will be made available to chaplains of other commands to the maximum extent possible. Facilities will also be made available to military members; their immediate family members listed in Defense Enrollment Eligibility Reporting System (DEERS); and authorized personnel for sacraments, rituals, ordinances, and other religious ceremonies—such as baptisms, weddings, and funerals—at which civilian clergy may officiate. When size and arrangement permit, areas may be set aside and kept permanently rigged to accommodate the private devotional needs of Marines, Sailors, and family members. The senior chaplain of each command prepares schedules of services that provide fair and equitable use of chapels and religious support facilities for the faith groups requiring facilities for worship and other faith group related activities. No fees or gratuities will be charged or received for the use of Government facilities in the performance of any religious act, sacrament, or rite. In addition, no fees or gratuities will be charged or received by a chaplain, RP, or Marine CA in the performance or support of any religious act, sacrament, or rite performed on Government-owned property.

It is the responsibility of the commander to upgrade inadequate CRP facilities and the construction of new facilities to meet identified CRP deficiencies. Command chaplains advise commanders on projects for facility improvements and expansion. The Chaplain of the Marine Corps advises the CMC on religious ministry facilities within the Marine Corps. In consultation with the MARFOR chaplains, the Chaplain of the Marine Corps also recommends special Chapel Life Extension Program projects, military construction projects, and priorities for chapels and religious support facilities.

Command chaplains will assist commanders by regularly inspecting facilities, thus ensuring proper maintenance of buildings and equipment used in the CRP.

Community Relations Projects

Chaplains assist the command in organizing and coordinating philanthropic activities in support of local communities and/or citizens. Such events often serve to enhance the image of military organizations in civilian sectors.

Authority to Sign "By Direction"

As the assistant chief of staff or principal staff officer for religious ministries authorized to administer the CRP, the command chaplain may be authorized in writing by the commander or commanding officer to sign "By direction" for the commander or commanding officer. This "By direction" authority is limited to the specifics of the assigned duties and responsibilities of the command chaplain. Per SECNAVINST 5216.5D w/ch1, *Department of the Navy Correspondence Manual*, "By direction" authority is conferred in writing and remains in effect until the officer is transferred or until rescinded in writing by the commander/commanding officer.

CHAPTER 5
CORE CAPABILITIES

Religious Accommodation: Facilitation and Provision

Facilitation

Chaplains and RPs manage and execute CRPs that accommodate diverse religious ministry requirements. Accommodation of individual and collective religious ministry requirements includes, but is not limited to, scheduling, coordinating, budgeting, and contracting. The RMTs will assess, identify, and research command religious ministry requirements. In the facilitation of religious ministry for all, the chaplain will address the following specific areas and functions:

- Identify authorized personnel to be served by CRP.
- Identify religious preferences of command personnel, as well as groups outside the command, to be served by the reporting RMT (i.e., other uniformed personnel, veterans, retirees, family members, contract personnel, and DOD civilians).
- Identify religious requirements. The process of identifying religious requirements (using a budget submitting office-approved needs assessment survey) includes personnel faith group preferences (identified in needs assessment), observance practices, accommodation concerns, and support needs. Command validation and approval is part of the process, as are identification of resources within and beyond the command and coordination of delivery of services within and across command lines in support of accommodation.

- Identify the accommodation of religious requirements. For identified and validated religious requirements accounting for operational tempo and mission activities (deployment, exercises, Fleet response plan, etc), develop programs and strategies to facilitate individual and group religious expression. Prepare a written plan for accommodation of religious practices and holy day observances. Account for scheduling, procurement of gear, consumable supplies, outside chaplain/clergy/minister support, and related support activities. Additional requirements include preparing for and briefing the command on policy and doctrine, with regard to accommodation in general and also specific accommodation issues identified for command personnel. Provide and promote an environment of understanding and respect for the variety of individual and group religious expressions.
- Organize religious services support. Execute a religious accommodation plan in terms of lay leader, other chaplain, civilian, and/or contractor support; facilities availability and upkeep; supplies; publicity; and related functions. Facilitate, schedule, and monitor worship services (that the chaplain is not able to provide personally due to faith group regulations) to include daily, weekly, special, seasonal, and appointed occasions, as well as funerals, memorial services, burials, sacramental acts, ordinances, rites, dedications, ceremonies, weddings, rituals, and other spiritual acts. Participate in organizing cooperative ministry with all RMTs to coordinate accommodation of the religious needs of all authorized personnel in a defined geographical or operational area. Identify,

assess, and liaise with civilian religious and community organizations in order to identify a broad range of religious opportunities that will enhance life within the military community.

- Implement the lay leader program. The RMTs will recruit, train, certify, and supervise implementation of the lay leader program in accordance with MILPERSMAN paragraph 1730-010. They will be familiar with faith group requirements and conduct lay leader recruitment, training, and certification. In addition, where access to religious services may be limited, they will plan and execute support for deployments, field exercises, and other operational contingencies in response to religious accommodation issues identified within the command. They will maintain a record of current and potential lay leaders by faith group.

- Identify and train volunteers (facilitation).

- Identify volunteers in support of the accommodation plan of the CRP. Volunteers may include choirs, musicians, altar servers, teachers, ministry group leaders, children's activities support, and readers.

- Consult with the command when command functions include religious elements (e.g., changes of command, retirements, history/heritage events, some memorial observances that are not explicitly bound by United States Code, Title 10). When command functions occur outside the context of the manner and forms of specific religious organizations, chaplains consult with the command with regard to purpose, audience, and expectations. Chaplains deliver appropriate support to the command function (e.g., invocation, benediction, remarks). Chaplains may abstain from delivering religious elements at command functions in light of faith precepts, without adverse consequences.

- Monitor compliance for "facilitate" capability. Systematically monitor and report volunteer, lay leader, contractor, and outside chaplain activities in support of all command religious accommodation efforts. Comply with DRRS reporting protocols and CRP and other inspection protocols. Ensure that subordinate command CRPs are reporting compliance data in the appropriate data collection systems (DRRS and Chaplain Corps).

- Measure performance for "facilitate" capability. Comply with all reporting requirements, to include data entry, recordkeeping, and Chaplain Corps data base inputs. Route and file reports as required.

- Facilitate ministry to the displaced and refugees in HCA and CA.

- Facilitate religious ministry to prisoners of war and other authorized detained personnel (see SECNAVINST 3461.3, *Programs for Prisoners of War and Other Detainees*).

- Plan crisis response or limited contingency operations as defined in JP 3-0, *Joint Operations*.

For supervisors:

Collect and analyze data on subordinate units as required and report to higher headquarters.

Provision

Based upon their professional credentials—ecclesiastically endorsed and commissioned—chaplains meet faith group specific needs, including worship services, sacraments, rites, and ordinances. Faith group specific needs include religious and/or pastoral counsel, scripture study, and religious education. Religious program specialists are uniquely trained to support religious accommodation. Provisions include—

- *Religious services.* Participate in cooperative ministry with all RMTs to provide for the religious needs of all authorized personnel in a defined geographical or operational area. Plan, schedule, prepare, conduct, and monitor worship services in accordance with the chaplain's religious organization's manner and forms. Religious services and/or occasions may include—
  - Daily, weekly, and special occasions.
  - Seasonal and appointed occasions.

- ◆ Funerals, memorial services, and burials.
- ◆ Sacramental acts, ordinances, and rites.
- ◆ Dedications and ceremonies.
- ◆ Weddings, rituals, and other spiritual acts.

- *Spiritual counseling and direction.* Provide faith-based counseling, mentoring, sacramental ministration, and spiritual direction (based on theologically derived truths) designed to enhance, grow, and strengthen faith, which positively impacts the spiritual readiness (e.g., develop character, morals, personal responsibility, community solidarity, resiliency, cross-cultural awareness, stress management, coping skills, grief processing) of individuals and groups of Sailors and Marines. Safeguard confidentiality.

- *Scripture and religious study.* Conduct group and/or individual faith-based instruction derived from the documents and practices of religious organizations designed to strengthen and grow people in their faith.

- *Faith-based life skills training.* Develop and deliver training from a religious perspective concerning marriage, child rearing, relationships, ethics, personal and spiritual well-being, crisis and suicide prevention, domestic violence, values, character development, and other moral issues.

- *Sacraments, ordinances, and rites preparation.* Plan, coordinate, deliver, support, record, and report faith-specific preparation, as required by religious organizations.

- *Faith-based relationship and/or marriage enhancement preparation.* Plan and conduct relationship enhancement and/or marriage preparation according to faith-specific programs (e.g., PREP).

- *Command functions with religious elements.* When called upon, deliver context-appropriate, faith-specific support for command functions with religious elements (e.g., prayers, hymns, sermons, memorials, ceremonies).

- *Outreach (religion-based).* Develop, plan, and coordinate programs to facilitate participation in religious ministries. Provide and promote personal and spiritual growth programs to include retreats. Identify and coordinate opportunities within the civilian community for the expression of religious and humanitarian charity by members of the military. Prepare and publish outreach-oriented religious communications for the benefit of military members. Plan and provide support to chapel fellowship programs. Participate in cooperative ministry with all RMTs to provide outreach in a defined geographical or operational area.

- *Capability compliance.* Monitor the compliance with DRRS reporting protocols. Comply with all CRP and other inspection protocols. Ensure that subordinate command CRPs are reporting compliance data in the appropriate data collection systems (i.e., DRRS and Chaplain Corps).

- *Capability reporting requirements.* Comply with all recording and reporting requirements, inspection regimes, data collection protocols, required surveys, including those of customer and command satisfaction.

> For supervisors:
>
> Collect and analyze data on subordinate units as required and report to higher headquarters.

Pastoral Care

Chaplains are uniquely chartered to deliver specific institutional care, counseling, and coaching, which attends to personal and relational needs outside of a faith group specific context. This includes relational counseling by chaplains, which is motivated by their proximity and immediate presence, distinguished by confidentiality, and imbued with professional wisdom and a genuine respect for human beings. Such counseling is most effective when based on strong relationships developed in the context of shared life in the same unit. Examples of care include deck plate ministry; counseling; coaching on military life; predeployment and postdeployment training for Sailors, Marines and their families;

crisis prevention and response; the CREDO program; memorial observances; and combat casualty ministry. Religious program specialists are uniquely trained and positioned to support the delivery of care, individually and programmatically. Pastoral care capabilities include—

- *Counseling.* Deliver relational counseling, which is based on the trust gained by a shared experience of military Service, characterized by confidentiality and mutual respect, and designed to develop and strengthen core values and personal responsibility in people whether or not they profess a particular faith background (e.g., walk-in, delivery of an ARC message, emergency leave, mentoring). Safeguard confidentiality.
- *Crisis response.* Pastoral intervention in any disruptive event in the lives of command personnel, singularly or collectively (to include care for the wounded and/or dying, and personal, family, professional, interpersonal, or other crises) for the purpose of offering support, advice, comfort, and/or referral. This would include preexisting plans that respond to mass casualties, natural disasters, and/or command emergencies. It also includes participation in unit/force/regional chaplain and RP duty watch bills.
- *CACO.* Specific efforts in support of CACOs and calls, to include initial and follow-up visits with the bereaved. Ongoing support for the command should be captured in other categories.
- *Deck plate ministry.* The RMT has frequent and regular participation in the daily life of the command, to include pastoral visitation to and presence in workspaces, at training evolutions, field exercises, and other such command functions. This ministry also includes visitations (e.g., barracks, hospitals, confinement facilities, residences). Safeguard confidentiality.
- *Crisis prevention.* Support of command prevention efforts in areas such as suicide, domestic violence, combat operational stress

control (COSC), substance abuse, sexual assault, and other identified areas that may arise. Support methods may include lectures, classes, talks, training, or other forms of communication.

- *Spouse, child, and family support.* Counseling, training, advice, comfort, and support programs delivered programmatically to spouses, children, and/or family members individually, as families, or in larger groups. This includes support for command organizations focused on spouse/child/family support such as Key Volunteers, spouses organizations, ombudsmen, United through Reading, Compass Program, and L.I.N.K.S..
- *Life skills training.* Assist the command in development and delivery of training and programs designed to address the unique stressors of Military Service by strengthening core values; developing character, morals, personal responsibility, community solidarity, and resiliency; addressing cross-cultural issues; and developing stress management, coping skills, and grief processing skills of individuals and groups.
- *Deployment.* Delivery of deployment support (e.g., predeployment, deployment, postdeployment, WT) to meet the physical, emotional, or spiritual needs associated with separation. This would include advice, comfort, and/or referral that is delivered individually and/or for groups.
- *Core values education and training.* Assist the command in the development and delivery of training and/or classes specifically designed to familiarize and strengthen commitment to Marine Corps Core Values.
- *Marriage and relationship enhancement preparation.* Delivery of marriage preparation program (e.g., PREP).
- *CREDO programs.* Support for the full range of CREDO programs to include planning, facilitation, publicity, and any other support as required or needed.

- *ARC.* Track and deliver ARC messages and manage the response system.
- *Command diversity initiatives (heritage observances).* Assist the command in development and delivery of diversity programs, including monthly heritage/history observances and special events.
- *DRRS reporting protocols for care capability.* Monitor compliance for care capability for compliance with DRRS reporting protocols. Comply with all CRP and other inspection protocols and ensure that subordinate command CRPs are reporting compliance data in the appropriate data collection systems (i.e., DRRS and Chaplain Corps).
- *Performance for "care" capability.* Track usage of care services. Comply with all recording and reporting protocols; inspection regimes; data collection, management, and reporting requirements; customer and command satisfaction surveys; and any other data calls.

For supervisors:

Collect and analyze data on subordinate units as required and report to higher headquarters.

Advisement

Chaplains advise commanders and other leaders on issues relating to morals, ethics, spiritual well-being, and morale; and also on the impact of the CRP on the command and command climate. Within the boundaries of their noncombatant status, some chaplains are trained to advise on the impact of religion on military operations. Chaplains also advise leaders at all levels of the chain of command in moral and ethical decision-making, cultural awareness, conflict resolution, and cross-cultural communications. Chaplains are supported in their work by RPs who are integral to the effort. Chaplains and RPs also advise on the following issues:

- *CRP impact on operations.* Assess the command and advise the commander and other leaders in the chain of command on issues related to free exercise and establishment of religion and religious accommodation—to include personal and family spiritual readiness, religious discrimination, and cooperative ministry across units.
- *Religion and cultural impact on operations.* At the tactical, operational, and strategic levels of war, advise on religious and/or cultural issues (external to the command) related to unit operations.
- *Conflict resolution (within the command).* Utilizing pastoral skills and wisdom, offer advice to leaders that enhances cooperation, defuses personality conflicts, and contributes to leadership effectiveness.
- *Moral advice.* Advise members in the chain of command on issues of right and wrong, fostering a climate of fairness, accountability, and trust.
- *Ethical advice.* Advise the commander on the ethical implications of command policies, decisions, trends, and situations. Provide advice to leaders within the chain of command on the ethical implications of leadership styles and strategies. Provide advice to leaders up and down the chain of command on ethical decisionmaking practices.
- *Morale.* When and where appropriate, suggest improvements to quality of service to include issues related to quality of life, quality of work life, human values, unit enhancement, retention, personnel, and family issues.
- *OCONUS COMREL (as part of theater security cooperation).* Advise the commander, as directed, as he assists the CCDR in development of community relations projects, which are components of the theater security cooperation program.

- *Religious leader engagement.* As part of the theater security cooperation program, assist the command, as directed, in engagement with local religious leaders to enhance communication and understanding (without violating noncombatant status).
- *Interagency.* As directed, assist the command in liaison with outside agencies (governmental and nongovernmental organization [NGO]), host nation, and civilian-military operations support.
- *Capability compliance.* Comply with DRRS reporting protocols. Comply with all CRP and other inspection protocols. Ensure that subordinate command CRPs are reporting compliance data in the appropriate collection systems (i.e., DRRS and Chaplain Corps).
- *Capability performance.* Track usage of services. Comply with all recording and reporting protocols; inspection regimes; data collection, management, and reporting requirements; customer and command satisfaction surveys; and any other data calls.

For supervisors:

Collect and analyze data on subordinate units as required and report to higher headquarters.

Guidance on Public Prayer

Navy chaplains who serve in Navy, Marine Corps, and Coast Guard commands are trained to distinguish between divine services and other command functions at which they may be invited to offer prayer. The United States encompasses a diversity of faiths and beliefs, as do the naval sea service communities. The policy set forth in DODI 1300.17 requires commanders to accommodate individual religious practices consonant with the best interests of the unit. Tolerance, mutual respect, and good order and discipline will help guide Navy policy, doctrine, and practice. Recognition that religious ministry in the military takes place in a pluralistic setting is a prerequisite for service as a Navy chaplain.

The DODI 1304.28 makes it clear that to be considered for appointment to military chaplaincy, RMPs must be "willing to function in a pluralistic environment" and follow the orders given by those appointed over them. Chaplains are encouraged to respect the diversity of the community as they facilitate the free exercise of religious rights protected by the Constitution and military policy, as described in DODD 1304.19, *Appointment of Chaplains for the Military Departments.* Chaplains may opt not to participate in command functions containing religious elements with no adverse consequences.

CHAPTER 6
COMBAT MINISTRY READINESS

Formation: Establishing the Religious Ministry Team for Combat Operations

The RMT is appointed and established to conduct religious ministry planning prior to combat; to support COA development; and to prepare the appropriate estimates, annexes, and/or other planning products for the unit. The RMT should be capable of developing, coordinating, and issuing policies, programs, and guidance for the planning and execution of religious ministry operations in support of combat. The team's planning should focus on the following actions by the unit chaplain:

- Identifying personnel manning and augmentation requirements.
- Identifying RMT training requirements.
- Identifying logistic requirements for equipment, supplies, and facilities, including communications and connectivity requirements, and RMT operational transportation requirements.
- Organizing, prior to deployment, how each RMT should plan, control, and monitor all religious ministry requirements in a combat environment. Specific tasks that require thought and planning and are paramount to successful ministry in the military setting include advising the commander on matters of religion, ethics, morals, and morale affecting personnel within the force.
- Coordinating religious ministry for a broad range of pastoral care, including memorial services, with subordinate RMTs.
- Coordinating logistic support for religious ministry.
- Having a thorough knowledge and understanding of facilitating religious support for enemy prisoners of war (EPWs) per MCO

3461.1, *Enemy Prisoners of War, Retained Personnel, Civilian Internees and Other Detainees*, which states:

"Military chaplains who fall into the hands of the U.S. and who remain or are retained to assist enemy prisoners of war (EPW), and restricted personnel, will be allowed to minister to EPW, restricted personnel, of the same religion. Chaplains will be allocated among various camps and labor detachments containing EPW, restricted personnel, belonging to the same forces, speaking the same language, or practicing the same religion. They will enjoy the necessary facilities, including the means of transport provided in the Geneva Convention, for visiting the EPW, restricted personnel, outside their camp. They will be free to correspond, subject to censorship, on matters concerning their religious duties with the ecclesiastical authorities in the country of detention and with international religious organizations. Chaplains shall not be compelled to carry out any work other than their religious duties."

- Providing, within the bounds of noncombatancy, informed advice on the impact of operations in light of religious and cultural customs, beliefs, shrines, and places of worship in foreign and host nation countries. The MCCLL will reinforce the need for RMTs to study and understand the religious and cultural aspects of indigenous religions prior to deployments. Deploying commands prepare classes for deploying personnel to ensure their awareness of cultural and religious issues and sensitivities. The RMTs need to be involved in the instruction of cultural and religious classes, or at a minimum, receive the presentations.

- Establishing and maintaining a liaison with chaplains of multinational forces. The AARs filed with MCCLL indicated that in large operational areas, and certainly in combat situations, a chaplain may not immediately have access to all his Marines and Sailors; therefore, the RMTs should be able to rely on assistance from personnel of other Services and faith groups in providing worship services. As authorized, this provision of ministry can also be extended to the troops of multinational forces, the appropriate civilian religious leaders, and NGOs, such as the ARC and other humanitarian/religious organizations.

Prior to deploying to the combat environment, command and supervisory chaplains should—

- Develop and verify ministry procedures that are consistent with unit policy.
- Coordinate appropriate training for subordinate RMTs.
- Consider provision of ministry and religious support activities and the scheduling of religious activities in relationship to the battle rhythm.
- Establish contact and coordinate religious ministry requirements with higher, adjacent, and lower RMTs.
- Understand where their unit lies within the chain of command and contact RMTs in supported, senior, adjacent, and subordinate commands.

Coordinated Efforts Between Commands

When an operational force is augmented, the supported commander's responsibility for coordination of religious ministry extends to his entire force or operational area. When possible, to ensure the best faith group coverage for the force, the supported commander's senior staff chaplain coordinates faith group support with the supporting commands. Chaplains are expected to initiate contact and work together to facilitate balanced faith group coverage and pastoral care whenever possible.

Component Religious Ministry

The increase in joint, interagency, and multinational exercises and operations has expanded the need for cooperation across Service and national lines. Emerging military chaplaincies are learning about cooperative ministry by observing how well the Navy/Marine Corps team and its RMTs work together. Cooperative religious ministry during combined operations can be coordinated to enrich the spiritual life of US and international military personnel and their families. Using religious ministry personnel from our allies can also enhance the cultural awareness of US troops. For coordination of such efforts, guidance is provided by JP 1-05, *Religious Support in Joint Operations*.

Planning: Develop the Religious Ministry Estimate Situation

When a unit has received a planning directive to develop OPLANs and COAs for combat operations, supervisory chaplains should begin to identify, coordinate, and integrate religious ministry support and efforts. Religious ministry must be tailored to the mission plan, the operating environment, and the religious ministry assets that are available. Religious ministry estimates should be developed in accordance with the mission of the unit and tailored in accordance with policy and doctrine to the type of unit. For example, RMTs serving with Marine expeditionary units (MEUs) should become familiar with the MCO 3120.9B w/ch 1, *Policy for Marine Expeditionary Units*.

Tasks for Command and Supervisory Chaplains

Receive Commander's Guidance

Once a unit receives a planning directive to develop OPLANs, the commander should provide guidance to the J-3/G-3/S-3 personnel. If needed, the senior chaplain in the force or unit should ask the commander for any guidance necessary to continue religious ministry planning.

Contribute to the Overall Mission Analysis

Command and supervisory chaplains should begin to review initial planning documents for religious ministry issues that will impact or be impacted by mission planning and provide input to the overall staff mission analysis. They will also need to determine the extent of RMTs available from adjacent nonsubordinate commands, develop and begin to track assumptions contained in OPORDs and OPLANs, and analyze the commander's mission and intent from a religious ministry perspective. In addition, they will need to determine limitations concerning constraints (what religious ministry must do) and restraints (what religious ministry cannot do).

Develop Religious Ministry Options for Courses of Action

Chaplains review the mission analysis and commander's guidance, and develop, at a minimum, brief COAs for religious ministry to support—

- Combat forces.
- Medical services.
- Mortuary affairs and personnel recovery platoons (PRPs).
- Noncombatant evacuation operations.
- EPWs, civilian internees, and other detained personnel.
- Formerly captured, missing, or detained US personnel.

- Civil affairs.
- Inter-Service chaplain support (if required).
- Host-nation support (if required).
- Religious leader engagement.

Analyze Religious Ministry Options for Courses of Action

Chaplains will provide religious ministry input into the COA comparisons. As much as possible, they should participate in determining the comparison criteria for the COAs. The best comparison criteria usually comes from the commander's intent statement; however, the chaplain may also provide criteria. By participating in the comparison of COAs, the RMT may provide informed recommendations to the commander that impact unit engagement:

Basic Predeployment Preparations

Predeployment Preparation: 6 Months Away

Personnel

The following personnel actions should be addressed 6 months away from deployment:

- Identify lay leaders. A thorough assessment of the religious makeup of the unit can be done through a statistical analysis of the command's faith group makeup. This may be obtained from the G-1/S-1 through a unit printout, or separate assessment and survey, 6-months before any deployment. The MCCLL recommends that chaplains contact persons of faith groups who may not have easy or any access to representative chaplains or clergy to ensure their religious needs will be met.
- Identify leadership challenges. The importance of self-care, care of the RMT, and care of commanders and senior personnel cannot be overstated. Chaplains, RPs, and senior personnel can fall victim to fatigue and combat stress just as easily as the Marines and Sailors they serve.

- Maintain the basic physical, emotional, intellectual, and spiritual disciplines that are critical toward keeping the RMTs in a condition to care for others.
- Obtain a SECRET security clearance for RMTs in order for them to establish and access SECRET Internet Protocol Router Network (SIPRNET) accounts.

Training

The identification of sacred or holy days in various religions that will occur during deployment and the collection of resources for those events is part of RMT training. It is important that the RMTs know and identify these special days when dealing with all religions to avoid the appearance of disrespect.

Note: If specific training is not available, resources for identifying holy days and days of religious observance are available from both ecumenical and denominational sources; but can also be as basic as Microsoft Outlook's® 'Add Holidays' option, which is available under the Calendar section. These, and other tools, should be acquired and catalogued for ready use during the opening stages of a combat deployment.

The MCCLL system and AARs have indicated that assigned chaplains and RPs should receive training in the following areas:

- *Pastoral care response to trauma.* The RMTs should read and conduct training on combat and operational stress reactions, posttraumatic stress disorder (PTSD), and trauma counseling (current resources may be found at the National Center for PTSD Web site). Additional training may be required to aid the RMT in specific assignments (e.g., surgical shock, trauma platoon [SSTP] training that is given at the Naval Trauma Training Center in the Los Angeles County Hospital, CA).
- *Combat stress and fatigue.* Prior to going into combat, an RMT must be trained to recognize signs for combat stress and fatigue. All RMTs

should become familiar with MCRP 6-11C, *Combat Stress*—particularly the stress continuum, stress decision matrix, and core leader functions.

- *Field memorial ceremonies.* Memorial ceremonies are a command responsibility and should be conducted according to express guidance from appropriate authority. Prior to conducting services, all applicable SOPs and appendices and annexes to OPORDs should be reviewed.
- *FRO and CACO training.* The FROs will receive all their training from MCFTB. This training should be conducted far in advance of a unit's deployment (refer to MCO 1754.6A and NAVMC DIR 1754.6A). The CACO training is handled by the Casualty Assistance Division and local decedent affairs offices.
- *Suicide awareness and prevention.* These presentations may be given prior to and during deployment. Resources are available on the Navy Knowledge Online (NKO) Web site in the chaplain's section. Another invaluable resource is the *Leaders Guide for Managing Marines in Distress*, which is a succinct guide for helping leaders manage their Marines and Sailors. To review this guide, go to the MCCS Web site.
- *Standard mass casualty procedure.* Provision of a rapid pastoral response is essential to diminish immediate and/or long—term negative effects of mass casualty events on personnel and overall command mission accomplishment. All available RMTs must be prepared—at any moment—to coordinate and provide immediate religious ministry and crisis pastoral care in a cohesive and reinforcing manner for all personnel affected by mass casualty events.
- *Mortuary affairs.* The RMTs must be prepared to visit mortuary affairs personnel and the PRPs in an assigned operational area. They must establish SOPs within the command and be prepared to educate subordinate RMTs on the requirements involved in ministry to Marine PRP personnel.

- *Interaction with NGOs.* Refer to the nongovernmental organizations discussion on page 6-10.
- *Grief counseling for evacuees.* The RMTs must be prepared to offer the appropriate grief counseling for evacuees.
- *Reuniting with significant others upon return from deployment.* Resources may be obtained through the MCCS Web site.
- *Warrior Transition.* The standardized COSC Program WT presentations may be found on the MCCS Web site under Military Life, Combat Operational Stress, and COSC Briefs (see WT postdeployment discussions on page 6-12).
- *Local religions.* A lack of awareness of local religious sensitivities could create significant problems with allies. It is imperative that RMTs obtain an understanding of the religious environment of the area of operations prior to deployment and entering a combat situation. For example, MCCLL from OIF I indicated some chaplains were not as prepared as they should have been to teach classes on and support the requirement for the religious and cultural aspects of Islam. A self-study course, such as the Middle East Orientation Course at the Joint Special Operations University, could have provided the required training and information.

Religious Program Specialists

Religious program specialists must address the following predeployment tasks 6 months away from deployment:

- *Embarkation procedures.* Establish a CRP budget that provides funding for religious programs and materials. For further guidance, refer to MCWP 4-11.7, *MAGTF Supply Operations,* and MCRP 4-11.3G, *Unit Embarkation Handbook.*
- *Marine Corps supply procedures.* See MCO P4200.15G, *Marine Corps Purchasing Procedures Manual,* for direction.
- *Tactical vehicle high mobility multipurpose wheeled vehicle (HMMWV) licensing.* Licensing must be accomplished prior to deploying. It

is imperative that RPs have their regular state driver's license as well as specific HMMWV licensing before a deployment. Religious program specialists serve as force protection for the RMT. It may be preferable to have a Marine driver for the RMT when in a combat environment.

- *Weapons qualification.* Refer to MCO 3574.2K for guidance.
- *CREST follow-on training.* CREST follow-on training occurs after "A" school or prior to assignment to a Marine Corps command.
- *Combat training exercises.* Participation in a training evolution that encompasses combat-arms exercises and training will develop religious ministry support skills required in a combat environment; for example, Mojave Viper training at the Urban Warfare Training Center, Twentynine Palms, CA.

Logistics

Recent MCCLL indicated that obtaining a dedicated vehicle for RMT transportation in theater is essential. If a dedicated vehicle is not available, arrangements should be made to share transportation with another section. In addition, the preparation, development, and maintenance of a 60-day mount-out box should be planned during this time. When MAGTF commanders receive operational objectives, they begin providing the MLG with estimates of supply usage and consumption. Staff estimates begin during mission analysis and are refined during COA war games. All RMTs must provide input to the commander's estimate. Due to the priority of critical and essential logistic requirements, religious ministry replenishment is slow and sporadic.

Chaplains should begin communicating with their respective camp commandants about berthing, office, and worship spaces. The RMTs should interface with their J-4, G-4, and S-4 about embark, fly-in echelon, and other supplies. Interface should also occur with the J-6, G-6, and S-6 about Non-Secure Internet Protocol Router Network (NIPRNET) and SIPRNET computer drops, phone drops, and access to message traffic. These interfaces are critical to the RMT for reporting requirements in theater.

For effective pastoral counseling, RMTs must maintain confidentiality. A dedicated space facilitates confidentiality and provides administrative spaces for the RMT. Often the provision of a dedicated space for RMTs means using a tent designated for another purpose, resulting in a shortfall within the unit. Each unit T/E should be modified to include standard equipment in support of the RMT. Ensuring that all faith groups are adequately supported during deployment requires ordering essential religious materials to support all faith groups represented within the unit, including their holy days, within reasonable limits (e.g., Qurans, Seder Kits, rosaries).

Predeployment Preparation: 3 Months Away

Personnel

The senior RMT of a force, regiment, or unit should ensure that deploying personnel in their supervision have up-to-date shots, gas mask inserts, and a 180-day supply of routine medications. All RMT members with dependent family members should file a family care plan with their personnel office.

All RMTs must be persistent about updating the faith group roster of those members who may be deploying. This includes the identification of all faith group needs and RMT assets necessary and available to support those needs.

Leadership challenge:

Senior and supervisory chaplains must continue to address the importance of self-care, care of the RMT, and care of the commanders and senior personnel.

Training

While legal briefs are the responsibility of the FRO, the RMT can play a vital role in supporting family readiness issues, such as childcare and custody issues, wills, and powers of attorney. Lay leader training needs to be ongoing and nearly completed. The RMT's training should be concerned with combat first aid training, radio communication training, vehicle usage, and training and orientation in the Marine Corps' supported activities supply systems management unit.

Since the deploying MAGTF chaplain will write Appendix 6 (Chaplain Activities) to Annex E (Personnel) for the deployment of OPLANs and/ or OPORDs, an important part of RMT training must include a thorough awareness of Appendix 6 for use in planning ministry and meeting reporting requirements for the deployment.

The RMTs should also continue to pursue cultural and religious training and study and the development of training classes for the troops.

Logistics

It is essential that the RMT's berthing, counseling, and location of personnel is current at all times. Furthermore, the RMT must ensure that all necessary items for provision of ministry are on the assigned unit's T/E. There are standardized allowances for the CRP. The RMT needs to be positioned where they will be best prepared to provide both a proactive and responsive ministry.

Providing effective ministry depends upon the RMT's level of mobility, and mobility in a combat environment is a must. Therefore, dedicated transportation must be available at all times for the RMT. The dedicated vehicle should be on the unit T/E.

In a combat environment, religious service participation by Service members dramatically increases over peacetime participation. One of the challenges of combat ministry is the uncertainty of the availability of musicians and instruments to enhance worship occasions with music. While MCCLL reports indicate that electronic music players are effective tools for increasing participation within the worship tents, findings are that worship DVDs, music CDs, and mp3 files played from a laptop computer or mp3 player are the most available and portable.

Communication

The keys to communication in operational religious ministry are information, location, accessibility, and reporting. Information is the content of communication. Commanders require accurate and useful information to make informed decisions regarding the levels of operational religious ministry required. During any operation, RMTs must be positioned where they are best able to provide responsive ministry to emergent needs and remain aware of the command's current status. The RMTs participate in the command communication loop by keeping their commanders and unit leaders informed of their movements and locations.

When the war begins, communications systems can become degraded or cease functioning. There is routinely no NIPRNET, landline, or cell phone connectivity with combatant units. The SIPRNET access is limited to key senior commands. To ensure each RMT has a radio and each member of the RMT is completely familiar with its operation, it is essential for the RMTs to coordinate with the J-6, G-6, and S-6. When using the commander's SIPRNET, chaplains should limit their communication to a "just the facts" basis via a situation report. Official business within the DON (including the Marine Corps) is via the Defense Message System (DMS). The RMTs need to familiarize themselves with the methods for sending and retrieving message traffic in order to communicate effectively with others. Video teleconferences, NIPRNET, and SIPRNET are valuable assets when the infrastructure is available.

Predeployment Preparation: 1 Month Away

Personnel

The following predeployment actions need to be addressed 1 month away from deployment:

- Validate deploying RMT roster.
- Provide the additional time-phased force and deployment data input, if required.
- Inspect deploying RMT personnel gear and equipment at least 30 days before deployment.
- Obtain legal assistance for last minute issues.

Leadership challenge:

The essential command requirement to fully staff, train, and supply the RMTs needs constant attention. Unfortunately, if RMTs have not planned for all areas of personnel support in advance of deployment, these areas will probably not be taken care of before the unit is in combat. Supervisory chaplains must continue to repeat the positive message of what the mission is and how the RMT is prepared to carry out that mission.

Training

Training includes delivering and receiving briefs. Combat stress (including suicide), ARC procedures, operational area religious and cultural briefs, and CACO are examples of briefs that RMTs should give. Force protection, tracking personnel casualty reports, knowledge of OPLANs and HCA procedures, reporting require-ments and note taking for AARs, and legal briefs on EPWs are examples of training briefs that RMTs should receive. Chaplains may assist with training for the handling of EPWs (and law of war classes) and work closely with CA personnel when such units and detachments are assigned to Marine commands. Training and supervision is necessary if EPWs are to be handled properly. Chaplains should be involved in these training evolutions and in the related law of war training classes.

Logistics

Effective RMTs plan and prepare for the next possible religious ministry task (short- and long-range) while taking care of the current need. Chaplains and RPs from higher echelons (e.g., MSC, MEF) make a critical difference in the effectiveness and morale of operational level RMTs by ensuring that they are resupplied and provided relief and assistance during sustained or extended operations. It is crucial that the units be properly supplied for the particular needs of their mission.

The RMTs should not solely rely on electronic means and Web sites to retrieve information while deployed. Hardcopy paper documents will prove invaluable as operations shift and RMTs are required to move to smaller units. Documents can include sermons, special services (e.g., memorial services, prayers, emergency ministrations, burial practices), and unclassified unit SOPs.

To ensure that adequate electronic equipment and religious ministry documentation and transportation accompany deployed personnel, the following actions should be taken:

- *Mount-out box inspection.* The senior RP deploying with the force, regiment, or unit should inspect all mount-out boxes of subordinate units to ensure that RMTs bring enough supplies for the entire unit for 60 days.
- *Office equipment/deployable computers.* Each RMT should ensure that they have protection from the environment for all electronic equipment and computers.
- *Transportation.* The RMTs must verify dedicated vehicle usage, berthing, and group and/or ministry tents with J-4, G-4, and S-4. To maintain operational religious ministry, RPs become the RMT's vital link for effective use of the command logistic support and resupply network. By maintaining regular liaison with the unit's logistic officer and supply personnel, RPs

ensure essential religious ministry supplies are included in the command's resupply network.

Deployment/Employment

The RMT, as staff for the commander, monitors, assesses, and controls the religious ministry support for the unit and directs changes based on the commander's intent.

The commander and his staff, including the chaplain, will control current operations and plan and direct future operations, including religious ministry. Religious ministry support includes a continuous presence for effective coordination and availability of religious, ethical, and moral advice. RMTs deployment/employment functions in combat are as follows:

- Religious ministry support includes ongoing training of religious ministry personnel, as well as a provision of religious services and activities.
- Counseling services, religious and ethical advice to staff and decisionmakers, and research on host nation and regional religious cultural matters and their impact on command operations are key to effective religious ministry operations.
- Knowledge of holy days and religious traditions is an invaluable tool for the commander. (see Predeployment Preparation, 6 Months Away paragraph on page 6-3).
- RMTs monitor religious ministry operations and the religious climate within the operational area for the commander.
- RMTs should continually assess the religious, ethical, and moral climate of their command for the purpose of updating command advisement, future planning, and training requirements.
- Continuously planning for religious ministry support enables the command to prioritize transportation assets for RMT use.

- Whenever possible, RMTs should coordinate transportation requirements and religious programs with other command activities. For example, RMTs can coordinate with the air planning board to use helicopters as "lifts of opportunity."
- Coordination and communication are critical to ensure that urgent ministry requirements are met through dedicated RMT transportation and joint operational area assets.
- Two critical elements of RMT operational mobility are—
  - Ensuring commanders and small unit leaders are informed regarding their RMT's location and schedule. Religious program specialists should always liaison with the unit J-4, G-4, and S-4 to obtain authorized and safe routes for travel.
  - Including RMTs in the communications network. The RMTs are best prepared to respond immediately to emergencies and crises when they are positioned forward, kept informed, remain in the communication loop, and have transportation immediately available.
- Senior and supervisory RMTs need to update current estimates of religious ministry by reviewing and confirming COAs in anticipation of ongoing operations and missions, advising, and disseminating adjusted plans and orders related to religious ministry needs.
- Proper planning includes synchronizing actions to established timelines and conditions and advising commanders and their staff in planning efforts.
- Senior RMTs must continuously support subordinate RMTs in their primary mission of religious accommodation, compassionate pastoral care, and command advisement. Religious worship services, rites, sacraments, ordinances, and counseling, are all a part of spiritual comfort, moral support, and encouragement to the troops. For example, MCCLL and ministry AARs from OIF indicated that memorial ceremonies are a critical activity in terms of effective grief and combat stress management,

potential impact on command mission, and high-event visibility within and outside the operational area. These critical ceremonies have become a command function that are overseen by the line, with the help and guidance of RMTs. Furthermore, these ceremonies have become standardized and demonstrate the importance in a combat setting of a comprehensive religious ministry plan, making worship opportunities and pastoral care available to all members of the command. Assets need to be coordinated by senior chaplains to ensure a balance of faith coverage, always being mindful of the limited supply and high demand assets (e.g., Roman Catholic, Orthodox Christians, Jewish, Muslim, female chaplains).

- Creative thinking and planning by chaplains will allow for dynamic on-the-spot worship opportunities, especially for small and dispersed units that are difficult for RMTs to visit regularly.
- Chaplains should develop—specially for hostile and combat situations—several types, formats, and lengths of religious ministry programs. For example, "hip-pocket ministry" talks, devotionals, scripture homilies, and faith group specific brochures or small literature guides:
  - Fear.
  - Courage.
  - Leadership.
  - God's presence.
  - God's protection, life and death.
  - "Going in harms way/through the Valley of the Shadow of Death" prayer.
  - Daily devotions.
  - Spiritual growth.
  - Thankfulness.
- Plans should also be made to support lay led or personal times of devotion for individual Marines and Sailors separated for long periods from their RMT or lay leaders.
- If an RMT is to minister effectively to Marines and Sailors in combat, they must be able to reschedule worship opportunities at a moment's notice.

- When a Marine asks chaplain, what's the good word, the chaplain should be prepared with at least one.
- Unit chaplains should have situational awareness regarding all Marines and Sailors in their unit. In a combat environment, MCCLL have shown that chaplains should be key players in the receipt and delivery of ARC messages. To allow optimal pastoral care, chaplains—
  - Arrange to routinely receive copies of all ARC communications.
  - Are routinely involved in the ARC notification process.
  - Are kept informed regarding emergency leave plans.
  - Provide follow up with all personnel returning from emergency leave.
  - Establish procedures that allow them to provide proper notification.
- Supervisory and unit RMTs must be analytical and proactive. They must proactively identify the religious, ethical, and moral needs of the command. RMTs should:
  - Research and interpret cultural and religious factors pertinent to operations.
  - Coordinate actions and/or operations where lines of authority and responsibility overlap and/or conflict in the operational area.
  - Ensure that any change remains supportive of current mission and intent, based on a continuing estimate of the situation.
  - Acquire and communicate operational information about religious ministry needs continuously.
  - Inform supervisors, decisionmakers, and other staff about factors that could affect a commander's decision.
- RMTs should collaborate with medical officers, health care, and mental health providers to coordinate the delivery of well planned redeployment briefs (i.e., WT and in-theater return and reunion targeted for single and married Marines and Sailors).

Note: After action reports indicate that return and reunion briefs delivered by the unit chaplain to his unit Marines and Sailors are often better received than those delivered by chaplains from other units. However, if the unit chaplain is not available, RMTs from other units with theater-awareness are better received than "outside" experts. The RMTs should coordinate with the unit FRO and their home base MCCS counselors to set-up spouses' return and reunion briefs.

Nongovernmental Organizations Support

Proactive coordination and positive working relationships with NGOs can enhance successful crisis response or limited contingency operations. However, it is the civil affairs officers, not chaplains, who are trained and prepared to affect NGO coordination. When directed, the RMT can establish and maintain positive relationships with NGOs, enabling commanders to identify possible answers for emerging support requirements that fall outside command resources or authority (e.g., support of migrants, evacuees). When working with civil affairs officers or public affairs officers, chaplains can assist commanders in matching resources with requirements. However, tasking RMTs with total responsibility for coordination with NGOs efforts can detract from their main effort to provide religious ministry to their commands.

The RMTs can advise their commanders concerning emerging religious ministry requirements and the need for additional NGO support when an operation involves evacuation or support of displaced persons. Early identification of support requirements that fall outside the assets, capabilities, legal restrictions, or limits of the force or command could prove critical in identifying and mobilizing NGOs and other resources. A chaplain's experiences and working relationships with

NGOs can be vital assets for the commander. When directed, chaplains can facilitate support and working relationships with NGOs on-site and/or in country.

Crisis Response or Limited Contingency Operations

Crisis response or limited contingency operations are typically limited in scope and scale and conducted to achieve a very specific objective in an operational area. These operations are generally part of stability operations and may be conducted as stand-alone operations in response to a crisis or executed as an element of a larger, more complex joint campaign or operation. Typical crisis response and limited contingency operations include noncombatant evacuation operations, peace operations, foreign humanitarian assistance, recovery operations, consequence management, strikes, raids, homeland defense operations, and civil support operations. During crisis response or limited contingency operations, RMTs will have a variety of roles to play in providing a ministry of presence, day-to-day out-and-about visitations (deckplate ministry), and advising the commander (see JP 3-0 for further guidance). Crisis response and limited contingency operations overseas will likely involve multinational operations (see JP 3-16, *Multinational Operations*).

In any setting—homeland defense, overseas, national, or multinational—decisionmakers may seek the expertise of senior chaplains; therefore, it is becoming important for chaplains to receive training in terrorist ideology and religious attitudes. Senior chaplains who have received joint PME and/or have some strategic level training and experience may be in a position to advise his commander in crisis response and civil support

scenarios. Training may be obtained from the Occupational Safety and Health Administration Web site and the National Incident Management System Community Web site. Additional training may be obtained from the Emergency Management Institute's Independent Study Office. The Naval Chaplains School also offers two courses that help develop professional competency in providing senior level oversight in crisis response situations—the Senior Supervisory Chaplains Course and the Strategic/Joint Chaplains Course.

Religious Support to Civil Affairs and Humanitarian and Civic Assistance Operations

The focus of civil affairs is to engage the civil component of the operational environment by assessing, monitoring, protecting, reinforcing, establishing, and transitioning—both actively and passively—political, economic, and information (social and cultural) institutions to achieve national goals and objectives at the strategic, operational, and tactical levels of operation, both abroad and at home. The DODD 3025.1, *Military Support to Civil Authorities*, and DODD 3025.15, *Military Assistance to Civil Authorities*, describe support of military units in civilian settings and situations. Much of this response addresses the calculated use of violence, or threat of violence, to instill fear or to intimidate governments or societies in the pursuit of goals that are generally political, religious, or ideological.

Military support and assistance to civil authorities is an area of emerging importance to combatant commanders. The United States Northern Command (USNORTHCOM) was established October 1, 2002, to provide command and control of DOD homeland defense efforts and to coordinate defense support of civil authorities. The USNORTHCOM defends America's homeland by protecting our people, national power, and freedom of action. Its specific missions are to—

- Conduct operations to deter, prevent, and defeat threats and aggression aimed at the United States and its territories and interests within the assigned operational area.
- Provide defense support of civil authorities, including consequence management operations, as directed by the President or Secretary of Defense.

The RMTs will play an increasingly important role in response to civil emergencies and disasters. Hurricane Katrina in the continental United States and Operation Unified Assistance tsunami relief in Southeast Asia were two such disasters where RMTs provided religious ministry in support of military humanitarian assistance operations. The RMTs should become familiar with the following publications on civil affairs and HCA:

- FM 3-05.40 (FM 41-10), *Civil Affairs Operations*.
- FM 100-23, *Peace Operations*.
- SECNAVINST 3006.2, *Department of the Navy Implementing Procedures for the Humanitarian and Civic Assistance (HCA) Program*.

Peace Building

Joint Publication 3-0 indicates that peace building takes place during crisis response and stability operations. The ultimate measure of success in peace building is political, not military. The RMTs play a supporting role in peace building through the sustainment functions provided to personnel.

When directed, RMTs in combat or deployment status have far-reaching opportunities to assist with NGOs, civil affairs, disaster relief, stability, and peace building operations.

Because peace and humanitarian relief operations appear to be a form of intervention that the US military will continue to undertake in the future, it is prudent to acknowledge the possibility that these particular missions may require chaplains to perform nontraditional activities. Chaplains can become constructive participants in the military/NGO interactions that characterize these kinds of missions. Participation of the RMTs in military/NGO interactions is just as crucial to the commander in strategic planning as that of the civil affairs teams. The RMTs should carefully evaluate their roles in these unusual operations, with the chaplain always mindful of the preservation of noncombatant status.

At the strategic and operational levels of operation, application of civil affairs operations or activities can mitigate the need for the application of other military operations in crisis response. The RMTs should plan appropriate responses for requests to join these efforts (see MCO 3440.7A, *Marine Corps Support to Civil Authorities*).

Postdeployment Programs

The RMTs will ensure that the command postdeployment programs target a wide-range of safe return issues, including the adjustment to redeployment stressors that are common (e.g., adjustments to life at home, changes in work locations and schedules, separation from comrades), and stress reactions that are cause for concern and treatment. The RMTs should become very familiar with PTSD signs, symptoms, and wide-range of assistance options, beginning with Navy medicine.

Unit classes should be developed, along with individual sessions for Marines and Sailors who are transferring, IAs who are demobilizing, and those who are separating from active duty service. The classes provide a forum to discuss both common and uncommon postdeployment experiences in a safe and helping environment. Pastoral ministry and making necessary referrals is the focus of the unit's RMT during this phase of postdeployment operations.

Followup postdeployment WT briefs should be planned and delivered 60—120 days after the unit returns. The recommended briefs are found on the COSC Web site (under Military Life, Combat Operational Stress, and COSC briefs) and focus on combat and operational stress reactions. The Web site's COSC briefs should be customized to include both inherent and outside local Navy medical providers, the Veterans Administration, MCCS, L.I.N.K.S., and the family readiness programs.

Marine Corps Combat Operational Stress Control Program

The COSC Program is mandated for all Services and combatant commands by DODD 6490.5, *Combat Stress Control Programs*. The Marine Corps has a comprehensive program to prevent, identify, and effectively manage stress problems. The goals of COSC are to maintain force readiness, contribute to combat effectiveness, and preserve and restore the mental health of Marines and their family members.

Combat and operational stress control is the responsibility of military leaders at all levels, with support from medical personnel, chaplains, and mental health personnel. Marine Corps coordination is administered by the COSC team in the Personal and Family Readiness Division, Manpower and Reserve Affairs Department, HQMC. The Marine Operational Stress Training (MOST) Program is an integrated package of educational

briefs, preventive interventions, and health assessments delivered to Marines throughout each deployment cycle—from predeployment through postdeployment. Two significant tools that leaders should be familiar with are the stress continuum model and the stress decision matrix.

One specific program, Operational Stress Control and Readiness (OSCAR), embeds mental health professionals, along with Navy psychiatric technicians and Marine staff noncommissioned officers, in ground combat units. The OSCAR program is based on the principles of community mental health, with the goals of primary prevention, early identification, and reducing barriers to appropriate care of operational stress problems. Chaplains may serve with OSCAR teams as a collateral duty and should acquire the requisite training.

The WT and return and reunion briefs are two components of the HQMC COSC Program that provide end-of-deployment normalization and education briefs for Marines and their spouses to prepare them for homecoming and reunion. Delivered by unit leadership, RMTs, medical personnel, WT, and return and reunion were originally developed by chaplains as programs of ministry to Marine operating forces and have been a major contributor to the COSC effort.

Indicators of the measures of the effectiveness of the Marine Corps COSC Program include the rates of suicide, divorce, domestic violence, end of active service attrition, and drug and alcohol abuse. Elevated indicators should cause the RMT to review the current program schedule and incorporate the needed adjustments. Further information on the COSC Program may be found in the MCRP 6-11C.

CHAPTER 7
TRAINING, PROFESSIONAL MILITARY EDUCATION, AND RESOURCE SUPPORT

Professional Competence and Training

A comprehensive training and PME program ensures that RMTs are prepared to meet the unique religious ministry requirements of CCDRs, military members, and their families.

Professional competencies are improved and expanded by PME. As a professional staff corps, the Chaplain Corps must ensure that its members maintain the competencies required by the PDTCs, PDTWs, PME seminars, and regional training designed to educate RMT members in the most current trends in institutional ministry.

Certain billets require specific professional qualifications identified as subspecialty codes. Billet subspecialty codes identify certain billets as requiring chaplains with specialized skills. A subspecialty is a Navy officer manpower classification defined by an operational, technical, or managerial field of interest, which requires specialized professional skills or knowledge. Professional subspecialty codes for chaplains and NECs for RPs are obtained through a combination of education, training, and/or experience.

Naval Chaplains School Courses

As Director of Religious Ministries for the DON, the Chief of Chaplains directs the professional development, education, and training of chaplains, Chaplain Candidate Program Officers (CCPOs), and RPs. Under the supervision of the Chief of Naval Education and Training, the mission of the Naval Chaplains School is to develop, implement, and evaluate appropriate curricula to educate and train chaplains and CCPOs.

Naval Chaplains School exists to prepare Navy chaplains for institutional ministry and professional leadership throughout and beyond the sea services. This mission is accomplished through a variety of resident, nonresident, and virtual courses designed to support chaplains throughout their careers—from preaccession to retirement.

Existing courses at the Naval Chaplains School are being revised to support emerging needs cited by commanders. The Naval Chaplains School coordinates the annual PDTC, along with numerous PDTWs, covering a variety of topics that meet identified training requirements. Current course information can be found at the Naval Chaplains School Web site on NKO.

Chaplain Corps Officer Training

Chaplain Corps officer training is designed to ensure progressive professional development, while meeting identified ministry requirements. Formal training and professional education begin with accession-level training and continue throughout each officer's career. The training and education system includes Navy officer leadership continuum courses, Chaplain Corps resident training courses, PDTCs, PDTWs, postgraduate education, local or regional professional military education, distance learning, and other training initiatives. The Doctor of Ministry in Military Ministry Degree is a voluntary program designed to further enhance the chaplain's ability for ministry in the military setting (visit the NKO Web site for guidance).

Emerging trends may necessitate changes in the delivery of religious ministry and require new training initiatives. When this happens, the Chaplain Corps develops the policy, doctrine, requirements, and standards to meet these needs. These become the basis for Corps-wide training. Once job requirements are established and training is offered, chaplains and RPs are accountable for meeting these standards.

The Naval Education and Training Professional Development and Technology Center maintains a database that records satisfactory completion of formal training courses. Subspecialty codes, additional qualification designators, earned degrees, and professional credentials are documented in each officer's service record.

Religious Program Specialist Training

Religious program specialists receive the training necessary to become, and remain, proficient in their skills and knowledge. In addition to qualifying to the unit's T/O specifications, RPs may be required by the command to complete additional administrative and computer training as needed. All RPs may attend the following schools:

- *Religious program specialist A school.* Computer-based training (approximately 20 days to complete) on approximately 25 topics, including religious accommodation, the supply system, correspondence, and the ROF.
- *CREST.* Provides expeditionary or operational training.
- *Religious program specialist F school.* 3-week, mid-manager (E5-E6) mobile course on how to prepare and conduct briefings, management of religious education, manpower, personnel management, writing correspondence, and facilities management.
- *Navy leadership continuum courses.* Navy leadership continuum courses required for advance in rate.

Training and Readiness Manual

All RMTs are encouraged to become familiar with, and use, MCO P3500.44A. The purpose of the Marine Corps Ground Training and Readiness (T&R) Program is to provide the commander with training standards for all ground personnel. The goal is to develop RMT knowledge, skills, and abilities for ministry in expeditionary environments. The performance standards are designed to ensure proficiency in core competencies. An effective T&R Program is the first step in providing a commander with an RMT capable of providing religious ministry in support of a unit's wartime mission. The T&R Program provides the fundamental tools for commanders to build and maintain RMT combat readiness. Using these tools, training managers can construct and execute an effective training plan that supports both unit and RMT mission-essential tasks.

Guidance for all training and evaluation in the Marine Corps, from entry level training at formal schools (such as CREST) to advanced PME for senior enlisted and officers, is found in what are called the cornerstone orders. All training and evaluation programs throughout the Marine Corps were designed and based on the guidance provided in the following cornerstone orders:

- MCO 1553.1B, *The Marine Corps Training and Education System.*
- MCO 1553.2A, *Management for Marine Corps Formal Schools and Training Detachments.*
- MCO 1553.3A, *Unit Training Management.*
- MCO 1553.4B, *Professional Military Education.*

Chaplain and Religious Program Specialist Expeditionary Skills Training Course

To meet increasing demands placed on the RMTs serving with the FMF, the CMC established CREST in 1996 to provide accession-level training in combat survivability, mobility, and field operations.

The mission of CREST is to train chaplains and RPs to provide effective religious ministry to Marines and Sailors in an expeditionary and combat environment. The CREST program emphasizes Marine Corps orientation, common combat skills, physical training and conditioning, field ministry support, religious ministry expeditionary logistics, and religious ministry support for Marine Corps combat operations. Navy RPs also receive Marine Corps Martial Arts Program training, weapons familiarization, and HMMWV permit instruction.

The CREST program is 35 training days (approximately 7 weeks) for RPs and 22 training days (approximately 4 weeks) for chaplains. Being a formal Marine Corps school, the Director of CREST reports to TECOM. The CREST program is presently collocated at Camp Johnson, NC, with the Field Medical Service School (East), where it receives administrative, logistical, and instructional support. The NEC 2401 may be awarded to RPs upon successful completion of the CREST course. Additionally, the NEC 2401 may be awarded to RPs who laterally convert from the Marine Corps (see NAVPERS 18068F, *Navy Enlisted Classifications*, chap. 4).

Command Religious Program Personnel Training

Trained volunteers are essential RMT members for many CRPs. Local training prepares CRP volunteers for specific roles within their local CRP. Chaplains and RPs are the primary coordinators for local CRP volunteer training. Volunteer training programs are developed with the same intentions as prescribed military training for chaplains and RPs. Training requirements, standards, and conditions for volunteer training programs are defined to meet the identified command needs for all personnel who serve the CRP.

Ecclesiastical/Religious Qualifications

Religious organizations require their clergy to maintain professional standards, competencies, and/or other qualifications that relate to their position as RMPs and the delivery of ministry in the military setting. These ecclesiastical and religious standards are met through continuing education units, annual conferences and meetings, and professional retreats and seminars. As RMPs, chaplains have the following ecclesiastical/religious development needs and requirements:

- Spiritual growth and renewal (retreats and religious conferences).
- Intellectual growth (continuing education programs).
- Preaching and teaching aspects of religious ministry (study and preparation as a part of the daily or weekly routine).

Individual chaplains must be proactive in pursuing their own ecclesiastical/religious development. Chaplains are authorized official travel orders for the maintenance of their ecclesiastical/religious credentials when such travel complies with the current DON travel requirements and restrictions.

Command and Staff College Distance Education Program

The College of Continuing Education (CCE), under TECOM, is the Marine Corps' college for supporting and advancing the new Expeditionary Warfare School for Distance Education Program (EWSDEP) 8650 and the Command and Staff College for Distance Education Program (CSCDEP) 8800. The EWSDEP course is generally for lieutenants and the CSCDEP is generally for lieutenant commanders or commanders. Successful completion of the CSCDEP will credit an officer with Joint PME Phase I credit and will help in future assignment to joint billets. Because not all officers have the opportunity to attend a resident PME school, the CCE delivers PME support to Marines and Sailors throughout the world via a network of satellite campuses. The CCE's main campus is located aboard MCB, Quantico, VA. The CCE satellite campuses are located at MCBs Lejeune, Pendleton, Hawaii, Butler (Okinawa) and Quantico; Marine Corps Air Station Miramar; and Naval Air Station, Pensacola. The seminar programs for both the EWSDEP and CSCDEP take 2 academic years to complete.

Joint Training

As joint training and education opportunities develop and expand, the role of chaplains and RPs will continue to be reshaped and defined. Complete integration of the RMT role in such training is essential for effective and efficient religious ministry for joint operations. Inter-Service dialogue and planning for integrated RMT training will continue to expand to meet the emerging requirements. As joint doctrine is developed and revised, the religious ministry requirements will be identified and defined. Cooperation between Service component commanders and CCDRs will facilitate training and preparation for the role of religious ministry in humanitarian assistance, disaster relief, crisis response, or limited contingency operations. Joint training is not so much learning new roles, but training Service-specific RMT ministry skills to meet joint and multinational requirements.

Fleet Marine Force Qualified Officer Program

The OPNAVINST 1414.6, *Fleet Marine Force Qualified Officer Program*, identifies the requirements for the Personnel Qualification Standard (PQS) for the Fleet Marine Force Qualified Officer (FMFQO) Program. Naval officers assigned to the operating forces of the FMF—MARFORs, MEF components, MARDIV, MAW, MLG, and MEU—may earn the FMFQO designation upon meeting all requirements prescribed in the cited instruction. Attainment of the FMFQO designation for a Navy officer signifies an achieved level of excellence and proficiency in Marine Corps operations. This designation indicates a fundamental understanding of a MAGTF and its components. The FMFQO insignia signifies additional general knowledge that enhances a chaplain's understanding and role in warfighting, mission effectiveness, and command survivability. The badge worn by Chaplains is distinguished from the one worn by the medical community by the absence of the crossed rifles.

Navy Enlisted Fleet Marine Force Warfare Specialist Program

All RPs serving with FMF units are required to qualify as Enlisted Fleet Marine Force Warfare Specialists (EFMFWSs). The OPNAVINST 1414.4B, *Navy Enlisted Fleet Marine Force Warfare Specialist Program*, outlines the specific requirements of this designator. The FMF insignia designates that Sailors have acquired knowledge that enhances their understanding of warfighting, mission effectiveness, and command survivability. The FMF designator is mandatory for all active duty E-1 and above personnel permanently assigned to a Marine Corps command and who meet the eligibility requirements set forth in the instruction. Other enlisted active duty personnel and Selected Reservists may qualify for the FMF designator if they meet eligibility requirement.

Armed Forces Chaplains Board

The Armed Forces Chaplains Board (AFCB) is comprised of the Chiefs of Chaplains and the

Deputy Chiefs of Chaplains of the Army, Air Force, and Navy and the executive director (non-voting administrator). The AFCB chair rotates among the Services, as does the assignment of executive director, who is the board's only full-time chaplain staff member.

The AFCB advises the Secretary of Defense—through the Office of the Deputy Under Secretary of Defense for Military Personnel Policy—on religious, ethical, moral, and ecclesiastical matters and coordinates religious ministry activities and polices within the chaplaincies of the Military Services (see DODI 5120.08, *Armed Forces Chaplains Board Charter*).

Naval Support Branch, Logistics Integration Division, Capabilities Development Directorate, MCCDC

Marine Corps Combat Development Command religious ministries doctrine officer functions as an action officer for doctrine development of religious ministries. In consultation with the Chief of Chaplains, the Chaplain of the Marine Corps, and the force chaplain at MARFORCOM (who serves as the proponent for religious ministry doctrine and publications), the religious ministries doctrine officer develops doctrinal products and distributes them to RMTs in the operating forces. This includes performing and providing coordination for the development of procedures, concepts, strategies, support items, and equipment employed in CRPs throughout the Marine Corps for the spiritual, moral, physical, and psychological rigors to be faced on future battlefields.

Additionally, the Naval Support Branch provides subject matter expertise and technical advice to the Chief of Chaplains, the Chaplain of the Marine Corps, the Naval Chaplains School, and the AFCB.

Training and Education Command, MCCDC

Located at MCCDC, TECOM functions as a training agency, providing support, personnel, facilities, and resources to the Chief of Chaplains in meeting training requirements and standards. The TECOM assists the Chief of Chaplains, the Chaplain of the Marine Corps, and the Chaplain Corps' Professional Development Officer (Chief of Naval Operations [CNO] N977) in the development, assessment, and administration of required training events as detailed in MCO P3500.44A. The TECOM also has Marine Corps Recruiting Depots at San Diego, CA, and Parris Island, NC; the MAGTF Training Command in Twentynine Palms, CA, and the Mountain Warfare Training Center in Bridgeport, CA, under their cognizance.

Navy Knowledge Online

All RMTs are required to register on the NKO Web site to receive the latest news items from the Chaplain of the Marine Corps and adequately manage their careers. Registration may be completed by logging into the Web site and following the directions.

APPENDIX A
COMMANDANT OF THE
MARINE CORPS MEMORANDUM

DEPARTMENT OF THE NAVY
HEADQUARTERS UNITED STATES MARINE CORPS
3000 MARINE CORPS PENTAGON
WASHINGTON, DC 20350-3000

IN REPLY REFER TO:

1000
CMC
4 SEP 07

From: Commandant, U.S. Marine Corps
To: Chaplain, U.S. Marine Corps

Subj: RELIGIOUS MINISTRY IN THE MARINE CORPS

1. Marines and Sailors in combat are our number one priority. It is through their tremendous sacrifices and those of their fellow service men and women that we will ultimately prevail in this Long War. The support we provide them must be world-class, and our Chaplain Corps is an integral part of this.

Navy chaplains have had a unique bond with the Marine Corps in a large part due to their shared sacrifice with their Marines. Our chaplains gain credibility by being in the field with their Marines, enduring hardships, and being "forward" in the zone — to be there when a Marine needs counsel or advice most. I think this principle is a vital part of continued service to our Corps.

2. Our Marines, Sailors, and their families must be mission-ready with spiritual, moral, and ethical maturity that is supported by innovative delivery of religious ministry and compassionate pastoral care. To this end, I have validated the four core Chaplain Corps capabilities articulated in our meeting July 3, 2007.

   a. Facilitate. Chaplains facilitate religious accommodation by managing and executing command religious programs that accommodate diverse religious requirements.

   b. Provide. Chaplains personally provide worship services, religious/pastoral counsel, scripture study, and religious education within their faith traditions.

   c. Care. Chaplains care for Marines and their families by delivering institutional ministry that attends to personal, spiritual, and relational needs outside of a faith group-specific context. Compassionate pastoral care extends beyond religious counseling. All chaplains must deliver a type of counseling, or coaching, which is motivated by their call to serve, distinguished by confidentiality, and imbued with wisdom and a fundamental respect for human beings.

Page number

CLASSIFICATION

d. <u>Advise</u>. Chaplains advise leaders at all levels on issues relating to morals and ethics, spiritual well-being, morale, and the impact of religion on operations. Chaplains are a critical part of the process where Marines develop cultural understanding and make complex ethical decisions. Cultural understanding and ethical decision-making are critical to warfighting and winning the Long War.

3. Chaplains are organic to our commands and remain trusted confidants in both war and peace. During our long, shared history, chaplains have effectively delivered unique and essential services. I have every confidence that your Strategic Plan is yet another step in the right direction and that you will be able to successfully carry out your intentions.

4. To fulfill the commitment we have made to our Marines, Sailors, and families, transform the Strategic Plan into action on the ground:

- Ensure your recruiting, accessions, training, detailing, and retention initiatives develop a Chaplain Corps that reflects the diversity in our ranks and among our families - pay special attention to shortfalls.
- Move forward by developing and implementing a performance measurement system that can be used to quantify value and identify and control costs.
- Stay engaged with commanders to support the development of training initiatives that promote ethical decision-making in all ranks.
- Develop a communications plan that effectively articulates this vision to all stakeholders and interested parties — both in and outside the Marine Corps.

5. Keep me informed as to your progress. In our next meeting, I look forward to seeing your proposed concept of operations and way ahead.

James T. Conway
General, U.S. Marine Corps

APPENDIX B
RESERVE MOBILIZATION PROCESS FOR RESERVISTS ON UNIT TABLE OF ORGANIZATION

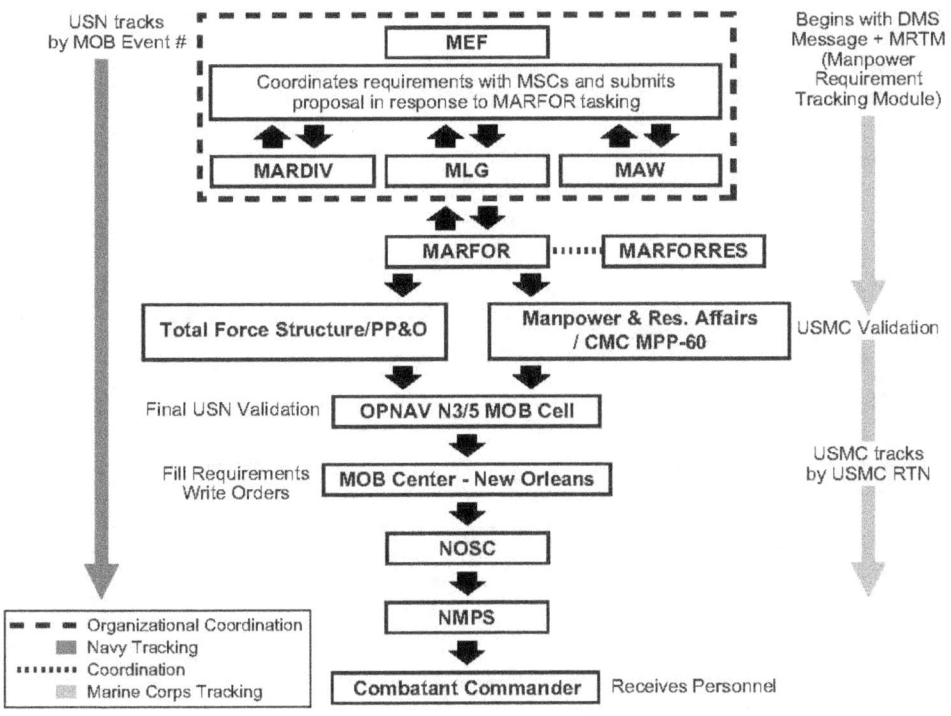

Key:

CMC = Commandant of the Marine Corps
DMS = Defense Message System
MARDIV = Marine division
MARFOR = Marine Corps forces
MARFORRES = United States Marine Corps Forces, Reserve
MAW = Marine aircraft wing
MEF = Marine expeditionary force
MLG = Marine logistics group
MOB = mobilization
MPP = Manpower, Plans, Programs, and Budget

MRTM = Manpower Requirement Tracking Module
MSC = major subordinate command
NMPS = naval mobilization processing site
NOSC = Naval Operation Support Center
OPNAV = Office of the Chief of Naval Operations
PP&O = Plans, Policies and Operations
RTN = requirement tracking number
USMC = United States Marine Corps
USN = United States Navy

APPENDIX C
SURVEY: US MARINES'
EXPECTATIONS OF OPERATIONAL CHAPLAINS

In this survey, conducted by CREST in March 2006, the ultimate goal was to provide chaplains the information they need to most effectively provide ministry to Marines and Sailors in combat. The CREST staff sought to evaluate expectations that Marines in combat had of their RMT. Combat Marines were asked to evaluate chaplain tasks as to their relative personal importance of application in the combat zone. The participants of this survey consisted of 62 US Marines who had been in OIF or OEF within the last 4 years. Marines were also given an opportunity to provide narrative input. See figure C-1 for a complete breakdown of survey participants by rank.

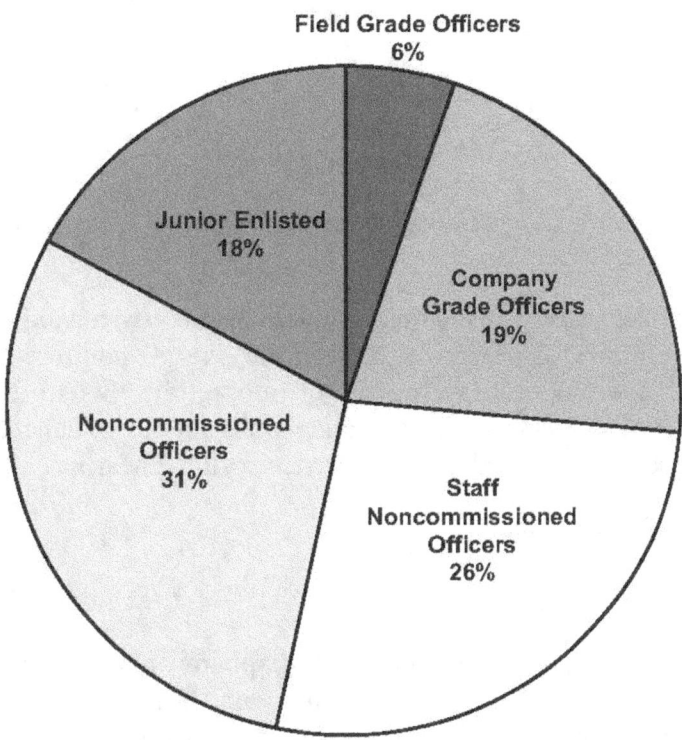

Figure C-1. Participants by Rank.

Interaction with Chaplain

Those surveyed also rated how they perceived the quality of their interaction with the chaplain. Most felt the interaction was positive or mostly positive, but 34% considered the interaction merely neutral. Figure C-2, on page C-2, shows that a very small group categorized their interaction with the chaplain as negative.

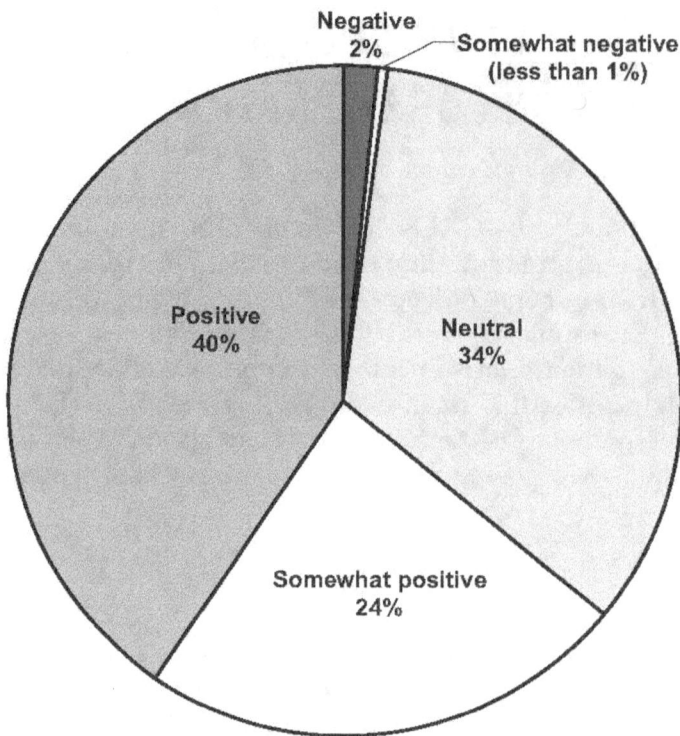

Figure C-2. Quality of Interaction with Chaplain.

The perception of the quality of interaction could be directly related to the frequency of interaction (ministry of presence). Given the overall positive attitude toward chaplains, tied to the moderate frequency of interaction, this study surmised that neutral perception of interaction with the chaplain would be enhanced with a greater frequency of purposeful interaction and presence with the Marines.

Specific Trends of the Survey

As a result of the survey, participants categorized the following trends as priorities:

- Frequent presence and interaction with a chaplain is a priority for Marines.
- The highest expectation for chaplains amog all Marines is to conduct memorial ceremonies to honor fallen comrades, followed closely by providing comfort to those grieving for wounded or killed comrades.
- Participants expressed moderate value for advisory tasks. These would include advising the command concerning such diverse topics as cultural awareness or suicide awareness.
- Encouragement tasks were of relatively lower importance to respondents.

Broad Conclusions for Ministry Applications

As a result of the survey, participants considered that the following conclusions were priorities:

- Chaplains need to be with Marines. The ministry goal of presence is to establish the necessary relationships with personnel in preparation for possible grief ministry following combat operations.
- In order to maneuver the combat zone to practice ministry of presence, the RMTs need to *train* to skills. Considering the high importance among Marines for memorial ceremonies, RMT training should also emphasize attention to this task.
- Knowledge of simple logistical procedures would enable RMTs to adapt ministry of presence to operational tempo. Chaplains assigned to FMF units would be well served to receive ongoing training in pastoral care.

GLOSSARY
SECTION I. ACRONYMS AND ABBREVIATIONS

AAR .after action report
ADSW. . . . . .active duty for special work
ADT . . . . .active duty for training
AFCB . . . . Armed Forces Chaplains Board
AMD. . . . . Activity Manpower Document
ARC. . . . . American Red Cross
ATP. . . . . .additional training period

BUPERSINST . . . . .Bureau of Naval
Personnel Instruction

CA. chaplain assistant
CACO . . . . casualty assistance calls officer
CCDR.. . . . . combatant commander
CCE. . . . . .College of Continuing Education
CCPO . . . . .Chaplain Candidate Program Officer
CMC . . . . .Commandant of the Marine Corps
CNO . . . . Chief of Naval Operations
COA. . . . . course of action
COMNAVRESFORCOM . . . . .Commander,
Naval Reserve Forces Command
COMREL . . . . .community relations
COSC. . . . . .combat operational stress control
CREDO. . . . . Chaplains Religious
Enrichment Development Operation
CREST. . . . . Chaplain and Religious Program
Specialist Expeditionary Skills Training
CRP. . . . . command religious program
CSCDEP. . . . . Command and Staff College
for Distance Education Program

DEERS . . . . Defense Enrollment
Eligibility Reporting System
DMS . . . . .Defense Message System
DOD . . . . .Department of Defense
DODD. . . . . . . .Department of Defense directive
DODI. . . . . . . Department of Defense instruction
DON. . . . . .Department of the Navy
DRRS. . . . . Defense Readiness Reporting System

EFM . . . . .Exceptional Family Member Program
EFMFWS. . . . . .Enlisted Fleet Marine
Force Warfare Specialist
EPW. . . . . enemy prisoner of war

ESORTS . . . . .Enhanced Status of
Resources and Training System
EWSDEP. . . . . Expeditionary Warfare School for
Distance Education Program

FAP. . . . . Family Advocacy Program
FMF. . . . . .Fleet Marine Force
FMFQO. . . . . .Fleet Marine Force
Qualified Officer
FRAGO. . . . . .fragmentary order
FRO. . . . . family readiness officer

G-1 . . . . brigade or higher
manpower staff officer
G-3 . . . . brigade or higher
operations staff officer
G-4 . . . . brigade or higher
logistics staff officer
G-6 . . . . brigade or higher
communications system staff officer
GCE . . . . ground combat element

HCA. . . . . humanitarian and civic assistance
HMMWV. . . . . high mobility
multipurpose wheeled vehicle
HQMC . . . . .Headquarters, Marine Corps

IA . . . . .individual augmentee
IDT . . . . inactive duty training
IDTT . . . . . . inactive duty for training with travel

J-3 . . . . operations directorate of a
joint staff; operations staff section
J-4 . . . . .logistics directorate of a
joint staff; logistics staff section
J-6 . . . . communications system
directorate of a joint staff
JMETL . . . . joint mission-essential task list
JP. . . . . .joint publication

LCE. . . . . logistics combat element
L.I.N.K.S. . . . . Lifestyles, Insights,
Networking, Knowledge, and Skills

M4L . . . . .Marine for Life
MAGTF. . . . . Marine air-ground task force
MARDIV. . . . . Marine division
MARFOR . . . . .Marine Corps forces
MARFORCOM . . . . United States Marine
Corps Forces Command
MARFORPAC . . . . .United States Marine
Corps Forces, Pacific
MARFORRES. . . . . .United States Marine
Corps Forces, Reserve
MAW . . . . .Marine aircraft wing
MCB.. . . . . Marine Corps base
MCBul . . . . Marine Corps bulletin
MCCDC. . . . . Marine Corps Combat
Development Command
MCCLL. . . . . Marine Corps
Center for Lessons Learned
MCCS. . . . . .Marine Corps Community Services
MCDP . . . . . .Marine Corps doctrinal publication
MCFTB. . . . . .Marine Corps
Family Team Building
MCMP . . . . . .Marine Corps Mentoring Program
MCO . . . . .Marine Corps order
MCRP . . . . . .Marine Corps reference publication
MCT . . . . .Marine Corps Tactical Task
MCTL . . . . Marine Corps task list
MCWP . . . . Marine Corps
warfighting publication
MEF. . . . . Marine expeditionary force
MEFREL.. . . . . .Marine expeditionary
force, religious
MET . . . . .mission-essential task
METL . . . . .mission-essential task list
MEU.. . . . . Marine expeditionary unit
MILPERSMAN . . . . . military personnel manual
MLG.. . . . . Marine logistics group
MOS . . . . military occupational specialty
MOST . . . . . .Marine Operational Stress Training
MSC . . . . major subordinate command

NAVMC DIR.. . . . . Navy/Marine Corps
departmental publication directive
NAVPERS . . . . .naval military
personnel manual
NEC . . . . .Navy enlisted classification
NESA . . . . Noble Eagle Sailor Advocacy
NGO . . . . .nongovernmental organization
NIPRNET. . . . . .Non-Secure Internet
Protocol Router Network
NKO . . . . Navy Knowledge Online

NOSC . . . . . . Navy Operational Support Center
NR. . . . . .Navy Reserve

O&M. . . . . .operation and maintenance
OCONUS . . . . outside the
continental United States
OEF. . . . . Operation Enduring Freedom
OIC . . . . .officer in charge
OIF. . . . . Operation Iraqi Freedom
OPLAN. . . . . .operation plan
OPNAVINST. . . . . Chief of Naval
Operations instruction
OPORD. . . . . .operation order
OSCAR. . . . . Operational Stress
Control and Readiness

PDTC . . . . Professional
Development Training Course
PDTW. . . . . Professional
Development Training Workshop
PME. . . . . professional military education
PQS . . . . Personnel Qualification Standard
PREP. . . . . Prevention and
Relationship Enhancement Programs
PRP. . . . . personnel recovery platoon
PTSD. . . . . posttraumatic stress disorder

RMP. . . . . .religious ministry professional
RMT. . . . . religious ministry team
RO. . . . . responsible officer
ROF. . . . . .religious offering fund
RP.. . . . . religious program specialist

S-1 . . . . . . battalion or regiment manpower staff
S-3 . . . . battalion or regiment operations staff
S-4 . . . . battalion or regiment logistics staff
S-6 . . . . battalion or regiment
communications system staff
SAPR . . . . sexual assault
prevention and response
SECNAVINST . . . . Secretary of the
Navy instruction
SIPRNET . . . . .SECRET Internet
Protocol Router Network
SMCR . . . . Selected Marine Corps Reserve
SOP. . . . . .standing operating procedure
SORTS . . . . Status of Resources
and Training System
SSTP . . . . .surgical shock and trauma platoon

T/E . . . . table of equipment

TECOM . . . . . Training and Education Command

T/O . . . . table of organization

T&R . . . . .training and readiness

UCMJ . . . . Uniform Code of Military Justice

US . . . . United States

USNORTHCOM . . . . United States Northern Command

VTU . . . . voluntary training unit

WT . . . . warrior transition

SECTION II. DEFINITIONS

assault support request—The method for requesting lifts of opportunity from operational area assault aircraft to move between camp and bases. Usually requires 3 to 7 days advance planning and approval.

clergy—As used in doctrine publications, refers to all professionally qualified religious leaders/ representatives endorsed by religious faith groups for chaplaincy in both the military and civilian sector.

Coalition—An ad hoc arrangement between two or more nations for common action. (JP 1-02)

combatant command chaplain—The senior chaplain assigned to the staff of, or designated by, the combatant commander to provide advice on religion, ethics, and morale of assigned personnel and to coordinate religious ministries within the combatant commander's area of responsibility. (JP 1-02)

command advisory task—A task to advise and provide counsel to the commander on personal, family, and unit readiness, including the religious ministry mission and requirements, morale, moral and ethical issues, core values, and religious ministry personnel, resources, and logistics.

command chaplain—The senior chaplain assigned to or designated by a commander of a staff, command, or unit. (JP 1-02)

command religious program—A program that provides religious ministry support that is planned, programmed, budgeted, and implemented to meet identified religious ministry support requirements. Also called **CRP**.

commander's intent—A concise expression of the purpose of the operation and the desired end state. It may also include the commander's assessment of the adversary commander's intent and an assessment of where and how much risk is accept-

able during the operation. (JP 1-02) A commander's clear, concise articulation of the purpose(s) behind one or more tasks assigned to a subordinate. It is one of two parts of every mission statement which guides the exercise of initiative in the absence of instructions. (MCRP 5-12C)

commander's planning guidance—Directions and/or instructions which focus the staff's course of action development during the planning process. (MCRP 5-12C)

confidential—The acts of religion, matters of conscience, and any other information conveyed secretly or in confidence to a chaplain or religious program specialist serving in their official capacities as a religious ministry team. Confidential communication may be conveyed through oral or written means, including electronically.

course of action—1. Any sequence of activities that an individual or unit may follow. A possible plan open to an individual or commander that would accomplish, or is related to the accomplishment of the mission. (Part 1 of a 5 part definition, JP 1-02)

design for ministry—A comprehensive document identifying a command's religious ministry requirements, mission, program goals, planned ministry objectives, ministry programs, plan of action and milestones, religious ministry budget proposal, a religious ministry spending plan.

free exercise of religion—The constitutional guarantee that each citizen has the right to hold, practice, and express the tenets of his or her religion or religious beliefs within the restrictions of applicable laws and military regulations. "Congress shall make no law respecting an establishment of religion, or prohibiting the free exercise thereof; or abridging the freedom of speech, or of the press; or the right of the people peaceably to assemble, and to petition the Government for a redress of grievances." (US Constitution, First Amendment)

joint—Connotes activities, operations, organizations, etc., in which elements of two or more Military Departments participate. (JP 1-02)

joint operations—A general term to describe military actions conducted by joint forces, or by Service forces in relationships (e.g., support, coordinating authority), which, of themselves, do not establish joint forces. (JP 1-02)

joint task force—A joint force that is constituted and so designated by the Secretary of Defense, a combatant commander, a subunified commander, or an existing joint task force commanders. Also called **JTF**. (JP 1-02)

lay leader—A volunteer appointed by the commanding officer and supervised and trained by the command chaplain to serve for a period of time to meet the needs of a particular religious faith group when their military chaplains are not available. The lay leader may conduct services, but may not exercise any other activities usually reserved for the ordained clergy. See also **combatant command chaplain; command chaplain; religious ministry team**. (JP 1-02)

lay-led religious service—A religious/faith group service conducted by a command-appointed religious lay leader. Lay-led services are not equivalent to divine services conducted by chaplains or ordained civilian clergy. Lay-led services are subject to chaplain supervision. Lay-led services constitute temporary accommodation of specific religious needs.

noncombatant evacuation operations—Operations directed by the Department of the State or other appropriate authority, in conjunction with the Department of Defense, whereby noncombatants are evacuated from foreign countries when their lives are endangered by war, civil unrest, or natural disaster to safe havens or to the United States. Also call **NEO**s. (JP 1-02)

operational area—An overarching term encompassing more descriptive terms for geographic areas in which military operations are conducted. Operational areas include, but are not limited to,

such descriptors as area of responsibility, theater of war, theater of operations, joint operations area, amphibious objective area, joint special operations area, and area of operations. (JP 1-02)

operational religious ministry—Those tasks and professional services performed by the religious ministry team in direct support of the Marines, Sailors, family members and other authorized personnel of the command to which they are assigned. It includes, but is not limited to, such religious ministry activities and programs as divine services, sacraments, rites, ordinances, pastoral counseling, visitation, religious and morals education, ethics education, critical incident debriefings, and advising the commander on religion, ethics, morals, morale and indigenous religions and customs.

operational religious ministry principles—The basis for the conduct of religious ministry in the Marine Corps: ministry of purpose, mission and focus of effort, planning, and mutual support.

operation order—A directive issued by a commander to subordinate commanders for the purpose of effecting the coordinated execution of an operation. Also called **OPORD**. (JP 1-02)

outreach task—A task to provide and facilitate programs that nurture, develop, and reinforce the spiritual development of service members and their family members, encouraging and enabling interpersonal communication and personal growth.

pastoral care—Broad spectrum of activities performed by chaplains to enhance the spiritual, emotional, and physical well-being of service members, their families, and other authorized personnel. Faith-specific ministry/sacramental acts are appropriate when conducting divine services and to individuals when consent is provided.

pastoral care task—A task to provide a positive influence by establishing relationships with personnel and demonstrating an interest in their lives. Frequently it provides opportunities to assist individuals who may be having any number of personal difficulties. It may include prayer or sacramental acts. It may include acting as a spiritual mentor to an individual Marine or authorized civilian according to the Chaplain's faith background. Pastoral care as a spiritual mentor is appropriate with permission. It is inappropriate without permission. Also called **ministry of presence**.

peace building—Stability actions, predominately diplomatic and economic, that strengthen and rebuild governmental infrastructure and institutions in order to avoid a relapse into conflict. Also called **PB**. (JP 1-02)

privileged communication—Communications to clergy held confidential as a matter of public policy and outweighing the government's interest in securing a criminal prosecution. The chaplain, the penitent, and even certain third parties present during the communication cannot be compelled to disclose qualifying communications. "Privilege" is applied when a communication is made to a chaplain in his/her capacity as a spiritual advisor or to a chaplain's assistant acting in an official capacity. Also called **clergy privilege; priest-penitent privilege; religious privilege**.

religious accommodation—To provide suitably or supply the doctrinal or traditional observances of the religious faith practiced by individual members when these doctrines or observances will not have an adverse impact on military readiness, individual or unit readiness, unit cohesion, health, safety or discipline. In accordance with SECNAVINST 1730.8B, accommodation of a member's religious practices cannot be guaranteed at all times but must depend on military necessity. Determination of necessity rests entirely with the commanding officer.

religious ministry—The entire spectrum of professional duties to include providing for facilitating essential religious needs and practices, pastoral care, family support programs, religious education, volunteer and community activities, and programs performed to enhance morale and moral, ethical and personal well-being. Enlisted religious support personnel assist the chaplain in providing religious ministry.

religious ministry and accommodation task—A task to provide and facilitate operational religious ministry, worship, prayer, spiritual direction, sacraments, ordinances, and/or practices of personnel to facilitate the free exercise of religion for the Marines and Sailors serving in the Marine Corps, their family members, and other authorized personnel. See also **free exercise of religion, religious accommodation; religious ministry**.

religious ministry plan—A plan that describes the way in which religious personnel will provide religious ministry to all members of a joint force. When approved by the commander, it may be included as an annex to operation plans.

religious ministry professional—An individual endorsed to represent a religious organization and to conduct observances or ceremonies. A religious ministry professional (RMP) is a fully qualified member of the clergy for those religious organizations that have a tradition of professional clergy or their equivalents. The religious organization's endorsement verifies that an RMP is professionally qualified to serve as a chaplain in the military and meets the graduate education and religious leadership requirements of DODI 1304.28.

religious ministry tasks—The six components of religious ministry that constitute the command religious program: advise the commander, provide/facilitate for the freedom of religion through religious ministry accommodations, provide pastoral care, provide religious ministry outreach, provide training and education, and provision of resource management (supervisory and administrative).

religious ministry team—A team that consists of the chaplain(s), religious program specialist(s), and other designated command members (e.g., chaplain's assistants, civilian staff, appointed lay leaders). Each religious ministry team's (RMT's) composition will be determined by the command's mission and table of organization. Each RMT will have a minimum of one assigned Navy chaplain.

religious program specialist—A Navy enlisted assistant who supports a chaplain in planning, programming, administering, and coordinating the command religious program. A religious program specialist is a combatant who provides force protection and physical security for a chaplain in operational environments. Also called **RP**. (This term and its definition are proposed for inclusion in the next edition of MCRP 5-12C)

spirituality—The expression of the spiritual nature in thoughts (forgiveness, mercy, salvation, thankfulness, etc.), practices (prayer, attending worship, study, charity, service, etc.), and relationships (faith community, the divine, humanity, etc.).

stability operations—An overarching term encompassing various military missions, tasks, and activities conducted outside the United States in coordination with other instruments of national power to maintain or reestablish a safe and secure environment, provide essential governmental services, emergency infrastructure reconstruction, and humanitarian relief. (JP 1-02)

supervisory and administrative task—A task to supervise the work and professional development of religious ministry and other command personnel (military and civilian, employed and volunteer) and other command personnel and to administer and manage the command's religious ministry mission.

training and education task—A task to provide and facilitate training opportunities, as required, for religious instruction and education, moral and ethical reasoning, spiritual aspects of core values, religious ministry personnel, religious lay leaders, personal spiritual development and personal and family readiness.

REFERENCES AND RELATED PUBLICATIONS

Federal Publications

Executive Order 13223, Ordering the Ready Reserve of the Armed Forces to Active Duty and Delegating Certain Authorities to the Secretary of Defense and the Secretary of Transportation

United States Code, Title 10, *Armed Forces*, Chapter 555, Section 6031, *Chaplains: Divine Services*

Uniform Code of Military Justice

United States Manual of Courts-Martial, Military Rules of Evidence 503, *Communications to Clergy*

Federal Acquisition Regulations

Department of Defense Directives (DODDs)

1304.19	Appointment of Chaplains for the Military Departments
3025.1	Military Support to Civil Authorities
3025.15	Military Assistance to Civil Authorities
6490.5	Combat Stress Control Programs

Department of Defense Instructions (DODIs)

1300.17	Accommodation of Religious Practices Within the Military Services
1304.28	Guidance for the Appointment of Chaplains for the Military Departments
5010.37	Efficiency Review, Position Management, and Resource Requirements Determination
5120.08	Armed Forces Chaplains Board Charter

Chairman of the Joint Chiefs of Staff Manual (CJCSM)

3500.03B	Joint Training Manual for the Armed Forces of the United States

Joint Publications (JPs)

1-02	Department of Defense Dictionary of Military and Associated Terms
1-05	Religious Support in Joint Operations
3-0	Joint Operations
3-16	Multinational Operations

| 4-0 | Doctrine for Logistic Support of Joint Operations |
| 4-05 | Joint Mobilization Planning |

Navy Personnel Manuals (NAVPERSs)

15560D	Naval Military Personnel Manual
15607C	Casualty Assistance Calls Officer Handbook
15839I	Manual of Navy Officer Manpower and Personnel Classifications, Volume I (Major Code Structures)
15909B	Enlisted Transfer Manual
18068F	Navy Enlisted Classifications

Navy/Marine Corps Directives (NAVMCDIRs)

| 1500.58 | Marine Corps Mentoring Program (MCMP) Guidebook |
| 1754.6A | Marine Corps Family Team Building (MCFTB) |

Secretary of the Navy Instructions (SECNAVINSTs)

1730.7D	Religious Ministry Support Within the Department of the Navy
1730.8B	Accommodation of Religious Practices
1730.9	Confidential Communications to Chaplains
1730.10	Chaplain Advisement and Liaison, January 2009
1752.3B	Family Advocacy Program (FAP)
1752.4A	Sexual Assault Prevention and Response
1754.5B	Exceptional Family Member Program
3006.2	Department of the Navy Implementing Procedures for the Humanitarian and Civic Assistance (HCA) Program
3300.2B	Department of the Navy (DON) Antiterrorism (AT) Program
3461.3	Programs for Prisoners of War and Other Detainees
5216.5D	Department of the Navy Correspondence Manual, w/ch 1
7010.6A	Religious Offering Fund

Secretary of the Navy Notice (SECNAV Notice)

| 1730 | Holy Days and Days of Religious Observance |

Chief of Naval Operations Instructions (OPNAVINSTs)

1001.20_   Standardized Policy and Procedures for the Active Duty for Special Work (ADSW) and One Year Recall (OYR) Program

1414.4B   Navy Enlisted Fleet Marine Force Warfare Specialist Program

1414.6   Fleet Marine Force Qualified Officer Program

1730.1D   Religious Ministry in the Navy

3461.1   Enemy Prisoners of War, Retained Personnel, Civilian Internees and Other Detainees

6110.1H   Physical Readiness Program, w/ch 1

Bureau of Naval Personnel Instructions (BUPERSINSTs)

1001.39_   Administrative Procedures for Navy Reservists on Inactive Duty

1610.10A   Navy Performance Evaluation System

Marine Corps Doctrinal Publications (MCDPs)

1-0   Marine Corps Operations

5   Planning

Marine Corps Reference Publications (MCRPs)

3-0A   Unit Training Management Guide

4-11.3G   Unit Embarkation Handbook

5-12C   Marine Corps Supplement to the Department of Defense Dictionary of Military and Associated Terms

5-12D   Organization of Marine Corps Forces

6-11C   Combat Stress

6-12A   Religious Ministry Team Handbook

6-12B   Religious Lay Leaders Handbook

6-12C   Commander's Handbook for Religious Ministry Support

Marine Corps Warfighting Publications (MCWPs)

4-11.7   MAGTF Supply Operations

5-1   Marine Corps Planning Process

3-37.5	Multiservice Procedures for Nuclear, Biological, and Chemical (NBC) Defense of Theater Fixed Sites, Ports, and Airfields

Marine Corps Orders (MCOs)

P1000.6G	Assignment, Classification, and Travel Systems Manual
P1020.34G	Marine Corps Uniform Regulations, w/chs 1-5
P3040.4E	Marine Corps Casualty Procedures Manual
P3500.44A	Religious Ministry Team (RMT) Training & Readiness Manual
P4200.15G	Marine Corps Purchasing Procedures Manual
1306.16E	Conscientious Objectors
1500.58	Marine Corps Mentoring Program
1553.1B	The Marine Corps Training and Education System
1553.2A	Management for Marine Corps Formal Schools and Training Detachments
1553.3A	Unit Training Management
1553.4B	Professional Military Education
1730.6D	Command Religious Programs in the Marine Corps
1752.5A	Sexual Assault Prevention and Response Program
1754.6A	Marine Corps Family Team Building (MCFTB)
1754.8A	Marine for Life (M4L) Program
3120.9B	Policy for Marine Expeditionary Units, w/ch 1
3440.7A	Marine Corps Support to Civil Authorities
3461.1	Enemy Prisoners of War, Retained Personnel, Civilian Internees and Other Detainees
3500.26A	Universal Naval Task List (UNTL)
3574.2K	Marine Corps Combat Marksmanship Programs
5311.1C	Total Force Structure Process (TFSP), w/ch 1
7010.17A	Religious Offering Fund

Marine Corps Bulletin (MCBul)

1754	Primary Duty Family Readiness Officers (FROs)

Army Field Manuals (FMs)

3-05.40   Civil Affairs Operations (FM 41-10)

100-23   Peace Operations

Miscellaneous

United States Navy Regulations, 1990

United States Marine Corps, *Concepts and Programs, 2008*

Paul McLaughlin, *The Chaplain's Evolving Role in Peace and Humanitarian Relief Operations.* Peaceworks 46 (Washington, D.C.: U.S. Institute of Peace Press, 2002), p.11.

Leaders Guide for Managing Marines in Distress, Marine Corps Community Services

US Navy Chaplain Gregory N. Todd, *Expectations for Operational Chaplains Among US Marines: Implications for Ministry and Training Priorities*, CREST, Camp Lejeune, N.C., March 2006.

Geneva Convention of 1949

Secretary of Defense Memorandum, Utilization of the Total Force, 19 January 2007